David Ropner
April 2003

The Ropner Story

The Ropner Story

Ian Dear

Hutchinson Benham, London

First published by Hutchinson Benham Ltd

Reprinted 1988, 1989

An imprint of Century Hutchinson Ltd,
Brookmount House, 62-65 Chandos Place, Covent Garden,
London WC2N 4NW

Century Hutchinson Publishing Group Australia (Pty) Ltd
20 Alfred Street, Milsons Point, Sydney, New South Wales 2061

Century Hutchinson Group (NZ) Ltd
32-34 View Road, PO Box 40-086, Glenfield, Auckland 10

Century Hutchinson Group SA (Pty) Ltd
PO Box 337, Bergvlei 2012, South Africa

Phototypeset by Wyvern Typesetting Limited, Bristol

Printed and bound in Great Britain by
Courier International Ltd, Tiptree, Essex

British Library Cataloguing in Publication Data

Dear, Ian
The Ropner Story.
1. Ropner Holdings — History
I. Title
387.5′0941 HE945.R59

ISBN 0 09 163810 0

Contents

	Foreword by Jeremy Ropner	vii
	Introduction	ix
1	The Teenage Adventurer	1
2	On His Own Account	9
3	Shipowner, Politician and Philanthropist	19
4	Peace and War	30
5	The Fleet Fights Back	39
6	The Great Depression	52
7	Tragedy and Triumph	65
8	Ropner's Navy	74
9	Taking Up the Fight	84
10	Victory and Reconstruction	98
11	Diversification	110
12	The Modern Conglomerate	121
13	Shipowners Still	135
	Appendix I: The Ropner Fleet	143
	Appendix II: The Ropner Family Tree	150
	Appendix III: Companies and Directors of the Ropner Group	151
Index		153

Foreword

The task of writing this history was quite formidable: the Ropner company archives contain very little material which can readily be transposed into a narrative.

Nevertheless, the range of sources from which Ian Dear conjured something to write was very wide and he spared no effort in his determination to discover as much information as possible and set the story in balanced perspective. Inevitably there was a plethora of material of too specialised a nature to be included and, equally inevitably, a scarcity of potentially interesting papers from the early years. Most of these were destroyed long ago and are beyond recall.

To the few surviving members of the third generation of the family who remember him the original Sir Robert was a remote, awe-inspiring and somewhat intimidating figure. He treated them with kindness but in those days grandchildren were perhaps rather more distanced from their grandparents than would normally be the case today. But it seems to me that a quality of humanity and generosity in Sir Robert does emerge from the text of this book. The success of the Company which under his control became one of the biggest and most profitable of its sort in the country argues the case that he was a singularly remarkable person. The fact that he was a foreigner with limited command of English and little money in his pocket when he first arrived in this country makes the extent of his accomplishment the more astonishing.

It is probable that the later years of Sir Robert's life were much saddened by the circumstances of the 1914–1918 war with his native country. Nevertheless such misgivings as he might have entertained were not permitted to dilute his patriotism on behalf of his country of adoption; it is evident that he had a particularly warm affection for the areas north and south of the River Tees (now Cleveland) where nearly seventy years of his life were mainly spent. He is, of course, the hero of this book.

It would be right to conclude this foreword by disclaiming any attempt by members of the family or employees of the Company to influence the author's view of the company's history, present position or future prospects. Other than where an attribution is made the opinions expressed are the author's own. I think he is to be congratulated on producing a readable book from the scattered and diverse yet incomplete material available to him.

Jeremy Roper

Introduction

THIS is the story of a company born at the height of the Victorian industrial revolution and still going strong in the microchip one.

Mere survival from one age to another is not all that unusual. What makes the Ropner story of such general interest is that, unlike most old-established firms, it has had a role to play in Britain's economic and political history. Not many shipping companies can claim to have sunk several U-boats during two world wars, which earned it the nickname, 'Ropner's Navy'. Or to have been an integral part of two major economic changes, when steam replaced sail during the last quarter of the nineteenth century and when oil replaced coal in the 1940s. Probably not too many could claim, either, to have been able to adapt to the post-industrial age, or to have combined the advantages of being a family-run business with the need, in these competitive days, for total efficiency.

Luck, of course, has played its part – at times Ropners has been quite amazingly lucky – but everyone knows how highly Napoleon rated that quality. Luck apart, the succeeding generations of Ropners seem to have complemented one another. Robert, the founder, had all the best qualities of the Victorian entrepreneur to start and expand a successful venture. The two sons who went into the shipping side of the business, John and William, were not risk-takers, but they had the faith during the Great Depression to rebuild the fleet after the First World War had all but destroyed it. And when William's four sons, Leonard, Guy, Jock and Robert, took over they had the acumen not to try to do the same when the Second

World War again nearly eradicated their ships. Instead, they had the business stamina to employ the same principles that had guided their grandfather: move when the market is down, consolidate, diversify into what you know, above all be in the right place at the right time, principles upon which their sons, David, Jeremy, Bruce and John, have been able to build, with the vital help of the non-family directors, a modern conglomerate that includes, besides shipping, property, insurance broking, garden watering equipment and high technology.

But this book is really about a shipping family who prospered by building up and running what at one time was the largest tramp fleet in the country – which prior to the Second World War meant the world. To generations of seamen the Ropner flag – 'the old bread and jam' – was a familiar sight in ports all around the globe. Many of them served in Ropner ships at one time or another, some during the worst of the Great Depression when a large proportion of the world's tonnage was tied up. Over fifty years later those times and the part Ropners played in them still provoke discussion, as one comment, printed in the August 1980 edition of the *Nautical Magazine*, from an ex-seaman shows:

There has been considerable discussion by M N A O A members in the correspondence pages of *The Telegraph* about whether the pre-war and wartime Ropners was a good firm or a bad one to serve in. All I can contribute to that discussion is one fact and one opinion. I served my time in a company not very dissimilar and we had a high regard for the efficiency of Ropners, which fought through the slumps to give much sea-going employment while lesser ones were collapsing spinelessly and ruining countless seafarers' careers. That's the fact, and now for the opinion. I reckon that Ropners was both good and bad, according to which class the employee was in. If an officer or man was competent, keen and an asset to the company, he was retained on the payroll and probably promoted; if he was incompetent, unkeen and a liability to the company, he got fired. Rough justice indeed, but it did ensure that Ropners' fleet sailed on while many contemporaries with their Masters, officers and crews fell by the wayside.

I knew one non-Ropner Master who was forced ashore to become a milk roundsman, another who lost all his savings in a market garden venture and another who became a prison warder. I'll bet that those three and many others only wished that they could get a job in Ropners. They would have called it a *very* good company.

Nowadays, financial writers think it is a very good company too. Ever since the early 1970s, when the diversification programme really began to take off, their columns in the newspapers have been headed with suitable nautical metaphors like 'Smooth Sailing For Ropners', 'Ropners Sail Ahead', and 'Ropners' shipshape profits' – and, occasionally, 'Ropner seasick'!

The economic climate has never been more difficult. Yet the present strength of Ropners and its record over the past 112 years just show what can be achieved even in the most adverse circumstances. It is a firm with a bright future as well as an illustrious past.

➳ 1 ➳
The Teenage Adventurer

THE story of any enterprise cannot be told in isolation from its environment. Ropners was born during an era of industrial expansion in a part of England that prospered inordinately well from the innovation of steam power on land and at sea. In 1835, ten years after the first railway, from Stockton to Darlington, had been opened, Hartlepool shipped its first coal cargo. West Hartlepool, where young Robert Ropner was to start as a shipowner some forty years later, had not even been developed at that time, yet by 1850 both places were bustling, booming, coal-exporting ports.

West Hartlepool's first shipbuilding yard, Messrs Pile, Spence & Co., was established in 1853 and it was here that the first local iron steamship was built two years later. Among those who took early advantage of the steamship was Ralph Ward Jackson, one of the most important pioneers of the new port.

Ward Jackson's main venture at West Hartlepool was the West Hartlepool Dock and Railway Company which established fortnightly steamship services to St Petersburg, and to Hamburg and Gothenburg. These ships eventually helped cause the financial downfall of Ward Jackson, but without doubt one of them, *Gitania*, did the port a service when she returned from Hamburg in 1857 with a tall, wavy-haired teenage stowaway whose head had been crammed with tales of the sea.

Robert Ropner had been born at Magdeburg, Germany, on 16 December 1838. His father, John Henry Ropner, was a Prussian army officer who had married Emilie Bessel. It is not known how many children they had, but Robert had at least two brothers and a sister.

In 1848, when Robert was still only nine, both his parents died of cholera and he was sent to live with an aunt at Helmstedt where he attended the local grammar school. His school reports show he was a bright pupil. Some sources say he was destined for university where he was to read theology. Robert, however, had other ideas about his future. He had immersed himself in the sea stories of Marryat and other maritime writers, and although he had never even seen the sea, much less a seagoing ship, he determined to make a life for himself in the merchant service. To this end he travelled at the age of eighteen to Hamburg. One account says he was with another lad and that both sought a passage together to Australia. However, the only Antipodean-bound ship in harbour did not have room for two, so instead Robert wangled himself aboard *Gitania*.

Accounts of how Robert got aboard the ship are conflicting. According to one source, he stowed away and was befriended by the steward, a Mr Luckhurst, who fed him and saw him safely ashore. Robert apparently never forgot this kindness and often visited the steward 'in appreciation of his favours'. Another account relates that he fell in with the chief engineer of the ship after the captain had refused him a passage. The chief engineer smuggled Robert aboard and he worked his passage as an assistant steward in the engineers' mess.

By whatever ingenious method he travelled, we know that Robert left his homeland early in 1857 and that the passage across the choppy North Sea cured him once and for all of any romantic notions about life afloat. 'I had a very rough passage,' he wrote many years later, 'and I was completely cured of the idea of going to sea, having moreover found that the life would not be what I had anticipated.' In another handwritten account of his life, which may have been coloured by the fact that it was written at the height of the 1914–18 conflict, he declared that he had left Germany because he had been opposed to Prussia's militarism and because 'I had read a good deal of the great position occupied by England and the freedom enjoyed by its people'.

Though obviously disillusioned about pursuing a career at sea, Robert must have found that England, at least, measured up to his hopes and aspirations, for he soon settled in West Hartlepool where he found himself, it seems, work in a bakery in the High Street near the docks. It was here that he met a girl a few months older than himself, Mary Ann Craik, of Newton Stewart, Wigtonshire, Scotland, whose father owned the bakery as well as a shop in the town. They married the following year at the parish church, Tynemouth, Northumberland, and in the course of time had ten children, five boys and five girls.

'I was married in 1858,' Robert wrote towards the end of his life, 'and to this I attribute, to a large extent, my success in life. Fortunately my wife was an accomplished lady with great tact, and she has been of the very greatest assistance to me during my life.'

Although he almost certainly arrived without any money – a Victorian ditty, '*The ABC of the Hartlepools*', described him in 1886 as R. 'the deep major – without the "half-crown" he has worked up the biggest fleet in town!' – Robert had received a good education. He had not studied English at school, but his aptitude at French and Latin marked him as something of a linguist, so it must not have been long before he became proficient in the language of his adopted country. Certainly within a year of his arrival he had made the first step in his career by joining Geipels, a local colliery fitter and coal exporter, where he worked as a junior clerk, not a position he could presumably have held without being able to read and write English well. His talent was soon recognized, and within a short time he was entrusted with a mission to Germany to extend the firm's business contacts.

At this period it was not uncommon for Germans and Scandinavians, attracted by a flourishing coal trade and by the lucrative timber import trade from the Baltic, to settle on the northeast coast. This influx played a large part in the development of the Hartlepools. Names like Trechmann, Nielsen and Herskind all contributed in some degree, though none became as pre-eminent as Ropner.

By 1860 Robert was sufficiently known locally to be asked to join the firm of Thomas Appleby, then trading as coal exporters and colliery agents, with an office on the Town Wall at Hartlepool. His job was to expand the firm's coal exporting business, and correspondence shows that he often visited the Continent for this purpose, and to good effect. It was said that although Appleby supplied the money Ropner provided the brains. The working methods of these two men are now impossible to recreate, but a letter from Appleby to his young protégé shows they were on the best of terms and reveals a little of how they conducted their business together.

'Dear Ropner,' Appleby wrote on 16 November 1863,

I trust this will find you soundly arrived at Genoa and in good spirits. I received a telegram yesterday from Carignani stating that he has sold the cargo to Brazilires at 32 and that one can charter more on the same conditions. I therefore set about finding another ship and hope to succeed in a few days when I shall telegraph. I also received this morning a long letter from him the contents of which I have not the slightest conception. He can show it to you and please ask him if he cannot write something more intelligible, say English or German. In fact if he can only make it between the two I could understand it. I think moreover there is nothing of great importance in his letter. I hope to have a letter from you in a few days and expect you will say you have enjoyed your trip. Nothing received since you left until this morning and I have chartered the *Mafate* with Treammason at £10-10s plus £1 for Hamburg and the *Palmyra* for Dieppe with Pyman at £9-10s. I see the *Antelope* in the bay. I don't know what to do with her in fact. There are no freights left. A Stralsund skipper's arrived this morning chartered (I expect with Ferrall), but he cannot find any orders . . .

At the same time as he began to prosper in business young Robert was improving his domestic situation as well. In 1861 he became a naturalized British subject and in the following years moved house several times to accommodate his growing family. In 1864 we find him negotiating to rent a house at Castle Eden just north of Hartlepool with all the acumen he must have applied to his business transactions. A substantial property was obviously necessary, for his eldest son John Henry had been born in 1860, followed by Emil Hugo Oscar Robert in 1862 and William in 1864. By 1867, however, he had moved back to the town to a house in Albion Terrace where his eldest daughter, Amy, was born. But this last move was perhaps motivated not by the need for additional space but by the wish to be back at the centre of things. For this was the year he launched himself into a second career by being elected onto the local council, a step which was eventually to lead him to a lengthy sojourn in the House of Commons. Twenty years later, when West Hartlepool was incorporated as a borough, it was

Robert who presented the council with its silver mace.

In February 1866 Robert became a full partner in the firm and its name was changed to Appleby, Ropner & Co. 'I visited upon you at Newcastle,' Appleby wrote to a colliery owner in the same month, 'to see if we could arrange for the factor shipment of the Shotton coals, but regret I could not find you there. Our Mr Ropner has just returned from the Continent where he has made arrangements for shipping that would at once guarantee a good trade at your prices for this year.'

With business booming the two men must have turned their minds to capitalizing on their success as coal exporters. When chartering ships much of the profit went into the pockets of the shipowners. Why not cut out the middleman and export the coal in their own ships? There is no evidence, but it is better than even money that young Ropner proposed this idea and pushed it through, and at the end of 1867 we find him writing to local shipyards to inquire about the price of a 190-foot steamer to be ready by 1 August 1868. On 30 December the quoted price of £11,500 by Messrs Denton, Gray & Co., who had by then taken over the bankrupt yard of Pile, Spence, was accepted. Robert's instructions were concise and specific. The new steamer was to be 'made as near as possible to *George Pyman*', a ship that had been constructed for a shipowner of the same name a couple of years earlier. And because steamers were still in their infancy the new vessel, in addition to her 80-h.p. engines, was 'to be rigged as a two masted topsail schooner with pole masts'.

The result was the 800-ton dw (deadweight) iron screw steamer *Amy*, which was delivered in July 1868. *Amy* has always been considered the first of the Ropner fleet and Denton, Gray's yard list names Amy Ropner as her owner.

Robert must have been as delighted to see his first ship as he had been the daughter after whom he had named her. But unlike Amy, who lived to be a hundred, *Amy*'s career was short and disappointing. Robert wrote to the shipbuilders on 21 August 1868:

We fear the steamer *Amy* will not come up to our expectation in carrying capacity. Nor will she carry her cargo according to agreement. It will therefore be advisable if you will superintend her next loading to satisfy yourselves on this important point. We expect she will be here tomorrow morning and as her cargo is all standing ready we expect to load her for the evening tide to get away Sunday morning.

Mr Gray will remember our first understanding was for £11,400 for 800 tons on 13′ to 13′ 3″ draft of water and we afterwards agreed to pay £100 more for higher depth of hold by which Mr Gray assured us we should get carrying capacity for at least 30 tons over and above the 800 tons as guaranteed. Since her first loading, we fear this £100 appears to have given us no advantage and which you will doubtless agree the particulars of her last loading is as follows: 696 tons of cargo and 101 tons of bunkers on 13′ 6″ by the bows and 14′ 2″ by the stern, the consequence of which was that we were not able to leave the port of West Hartlepool last Thursday night. Had she been not more than 13′ 3″ we could have got safely to sea that tide.

Amy's second loading proved equally unsatisfactory, but before the problem could be resolved she stranded at Winga in the Grecian Archipeligo and had to be abandoned. This tragedy, however, did not deter Robert in his ambitions to build up a fleet of steamers. The introduction of the steamer, with its greater reliability, stability and safety, had brought with it limitless business opportunities and, although by today's standards the loss of vessels, and sometimes life, was appallingly high, the statistics were a great improvement over the days of commercial sail.

Nor did the failure of *Amy* to come up to her builders' expectations sour Robert's relationship with Denton, Gray, for he was soon contracting for a second ship, a 1000-tonner 'to be ready for sea 1 May 1870'. In fact, Denton, Gray and then William Gray built many ships over the years for Ropners, and the two families were brought even closer when Robert's grandson, Guy, married William Gray's granddaughter, Margarita, in 1921.

Two ships were delivered in 1870: *Magdala* in April and *Shotton* in October. (In May a 1205-ton dw steamer called *May*, which Denton, Gray's yard list notes was also ordered by Appleby, Ropner in October 1869, was launched too, but the records show that by that time Robert had no financial interest in her.) In all probability both these were owned in the same proportion as *Amy* by the partners, that is 24/64ths each, the balance being bought initially by the builders as a kind of hire-purchase arrangement. *Seaton* (April 1871), *Magdeburg* (August 1871), *Wave* (October 1871), *Hardwick* (June 1873) and *Breeze* (1874) were almost certainly owned in the same proportions as well, the contract having been in the firm's name. However, in 1871 Robert contracted to have his first ship built in his own name. Constructed by William Gray, *Lufra* was launched in July 1872 and was subsequently managed by Appleby, Ropner, Robert selling 6/64ths to Appleby and retaining 20/64ths himself.

The Merchant Shipping Act of 1854 had introduced the 'sixty-fourths' system of owning and trading a vessel. Under it the cost of a ship, and subsequently her profits, were divided into sixty-four parts, each of which could be sold to a different person. The ship was then traded on her own account and the profits were divided proportionately amongst the shareholders, the 'sixty-fourthers' as they were called, after costs and commissions had been deducted. However, shareholders were also responsible for debts, repairs and collision expenses which were not covered by insurance and a 'call' could be made on them for these. Good management, therefore, was of paramount importance. Shareholders came from many different backgrounds, but were mostly local people. Robert, after starting out on his own, had substantial backing from a number of local businesses and from the Lancashire and West Riding textile manufacturers, but he also offered shares to business acquaintances and neighbours, who were soon all too eager to take them up.

'Next year will be a first rate year for steamers,' Robert wrote to a Mr James Read of Sunderland offering him 11/64ths of *Magdala*, 'as such a quantity of railway iron has to go to Cronstadt and we know of boats who have cleared 20% in two voyages to Cronstadt this autumn.'

Robert proved to be absolutely correct in his predictions and on 17 October 1870 he was able to write to another shareholder: 'We have pleasure to inform you that the steamer *Magdala* has been very fortunate in completing her voyages since 24 April and has left a profit of about 25% for six months ending 24th of this month.'

By the end of that year *Magdala* had made 34 per cent in eight months of trading.

Although Robert had his steamers built rather larger than most, between 2000 and 3000 tons deadweight, such was the pressure of business that in December 1873 he was writing to Short Bros. at Sunderland to inquire whether they had any steamers built but unsold.

Correspondence of that period also reveals that Robert negotiated the lease of Hardwick Hall, Castle Eden, in the summer of 1872 and that in August 1873 their Newcastle office was closed 'as it was impossible for either partner ever to get to Newcastle because of the pressure of business.' The same month Robert wrote to a shareholder of *Hardwick* that 'I think we shall have a very fair half year with all the boats. The prospects are good.'

The prospects for Robert, however, were more than good. As a young man of thirty-five he had the world at his feet, and one suspects that he probably knew it. Yet by all accounts he was a modest, unassuming man who liked nothing better than to walk down to the docks and listen to the yarns of sailors from his homeland. He lived frugally and worked hard. In none of his correspondence or later in his public utterances was there ever a hint of exaggeration. He was a down-to-earth man who did not mince his words, using understatement and a dry humour to get across what he wanted to say. When he moved to Hardwick Hall he did not leave his office for lunch. Instead, he stayed at his desk and ate sandwiches and drank cold water.

A contemporary photograph confirms a description of him as having a 'tall erect figure, fine wavy hair, fresh complexion and well-cut features'. He stands leaning lightly on a chair, an elegant, graceful man, just over six feet tall, slim and upstanding. His face is shrouded in a handsome beard and moustache, and from under slightly arched eyebrows his eyes gaze steadily out at the world with a piercing look. You get the impression it would be difficult to pull any wool over them.

By 1874 he was a respected member of Hartlepool town council of some seven years' standing and had begun to broaden his political horizons by assisting at the different elections in South Durham. He now lived in an imposing residence and, with the birth of Walter in 1868, Leonard in 1873 and Lilian in 1874, his family had grown to five boys and two girls. In addition, in these early years he was an active Freemason and was Worshipful Master of St Helen's Lodge in 1876. Last but not least, his business acumen and foresight had been proven during fifteen years of hard work. The time had come to move on.

2
On His Own Account

THERE is no record of why Robert struck out on his own, only a series of letters to Appleby which on occasions sound sharp but by no means angry. 'Surprised and aggrieved' is the strongest phrase in them and on the whole one gets the impression that the termination of the partnership was tersely conducted but without lasting rancour. Certainly Robert later asserted that they parted 'by mutual consent' and that 'we have always been good friends, never having had any difference whatever, and the good friendship has continued up to this day.'

Probably Robert, being a man of initiative and drive, simply wanted to be his own boss. Almost certainly Appleby was not as dynamic, and this may have caused friction when it came to assessing a business deal. However it occurred, by the middle of 1874 Robert was negotiating with a Captain Young to command a ship on his own account which he obviously intended to manage himself. *Renpor* was due to be completed in July and Robert wrote to Young that the ship 'is mine not the firm's', a fact the captain would have quickly established if he did crossword puzzles as Renpor is an anagram of Ropner. Young was offered 14d a day if his references were satisfactory.

Soon afterwards negotiations began for the termination of the partnership and in November it was agreed that it would cease at the end of the year. It was decided to split the steamers between the partners and apparently each captain was asked with which partner he would prefer to stay. *Shotton*, *Magdeburg*, *Seaton*, *Wave* and, of course, *Lufra* came under Robert's control. (*Magdala*, always counted as a Ropner ship, had been wrecked while on passage from St Petersburg to London in October 1872.) Robert had made many friends amongst the captains, including Brackenbury, Rooke and Granger, so it is not surprising that the majority preferred to stay with him. Rooke had been captain of *Amy* when she foundered and Robert later made him marine superintendent.

The transfer of some of these ships took place before the partnership was officially dissolved. A letter reveals this when some years later a dispute arose as to the division of profits of a coal cargo shipped in *Wave* to London during December 1874. Robert wrote that *Wave* had become his property on 18 November 1874 and that the profits therefore belonged to him. The disagreement arose because Appleby tried to claim half the profits of this shipment by invoking the deed of agreement both men had drawn up in 1866 when they had become partners. This stated that Robert could not start up as a coal exporter on his own or with anyone else, and Appleby claimed that Robert had infringed this clause by the *Wave* shipment. To this Robert retorted that he had not exported coal but had simply sold it in London, and that anyway the deed was invalid as it could not have covered the contingencies raised by the dispute as at the time of the deed the firm had not owned any ships.

The letter also reveals something of the way the partnership was run. Robert wrote:

> I only received 2/5ths [of the profits] and Mr Appleby 3/5ths for the first two years. Both he and I frequently bought and sold far beyond the amount stipulated in the Deed without the written consent of each other and contributed each one half of any bad debt incurred, either by one or the other, without the other's consent. The style of the firm was altered to Appleby, Ropner and Co. and the capital was increased to £10,000, viz: £5000 each. All this was done, I admit, by mutual consent, but this very fact proves that the Deed of Partnership was superseded by verbal arrangements and cannot now be invoked by Mr Appleby for a particular purpose.

Other minor irritations arose between the two men in the years immediately following their separation, but they must have been amicably solved for there was no recourse to the law. Certainly they continued to do business together as Robert sold Appleby *Magdeburg* and *Shotton* in 1877.

On 2 January 1875 Robert wrote to his clients: 'The partnership between Mr Thomas Appleby and myself having been dissolved I beg to inform you that I shall continue the business of Merchants and Shipowners under the style of R. Ropner and Company and I hope to be favoured with a continuance of your valued confidence.'

It was a bold step for any young man to take for although the possibility of high profits was present the risks were also formidable. Of the six ships (for they also included *Renpor*) under his control only one, *Seaton*, survived the sea to be broken up. *Shotton*, when under Swedish ownership, was abandoned in the North Atlantic in 1889; *Magdeburg*, while still owned by Appleby, was wrecked in 1886; *Lufra* had to be abandoned in the Bay of Biscay in 1879; and *Renpor* was sunk by pack ice in the North Atlantic in 1882.

The extent of such casualties was by no means unusual during this era, and though total loss would have been covered, probably at first through the North of England Steamship Insurance Association and certainly by Lloyds later on, the many other risks inherent in running a shipping company were often covered by the shipowners themselves. They did this by banding together to form various insurance clubs by which risks were mutually shared. The North of England Protecting Club, formed in 1860, was one such organization, while the North of England Indemnity Association was another. Later these combined to become the North of England P. & I. (Protection and Indemnity) Association in which Ropner ships are still entered. Robert served his time as chairman of this association, as did one of his sons, two of his grandsons and one of his great-grandsons. However, when Robert had built up his fleet he saw no reason to pay unnecessary premiums. He therefore started his own particular average (for partial damage, not total loss) fund so that damage to one ship was shared by them all. This fund was continued until 1955 when the sharp drop in the number of ships in the fleet combined with the spiralling costs of repairs to make it uneconomic to continue any form of self-insurance.

A letter from Robert to HM Consul in Alexandria in August 1875 also shows that running a profitable business was not always an easy matter. In it Robert informed the consul that his confidential clerk was on his way to Alexandria to reclaim the sum of £1766 12s 7d owed to him by a Mr Charles Grace.

On the whole, though, Robert thrived, this being partly due perhaps to the fact that he had been able to retain the agency of the Haswell, Shotton and Easington Coal Company. Certainly by the end of his first year on his own he was sufficiently confident of the future of his business to engage another clerk, a John C. Thwaites, at £110 per annum. Thwaites stayed with the firm all his life, as did so many Ropner employees in the following years. Charles Ringwood, for instance, finally retired in 1976, some sixty years after he first joined the company. Thwaites eventually became the Company Secretary and there are one or two members of the firm still alive who recall working with him.

The next five years must have been both hectic and fruitful. In 1874, in addition to his own business commitments, Robert took on the task of commanding the Castle Eden Volunteers, a company of the 16th Durham Light Infantry, a post he held until 1878 with the rank of major. He eventually rose to the rank of colonel in the 1st Durham Volunteer Regiment and received the Volunteer Decoration for long service. Two more daughters, Eveline (1876) and Mabel (1877), joined the family (Elsa, the last, was born in 1886), and during these years he also began gradually to build up his fleet of steamers for the Baltic and Far East trades. So dominant did he become in the former that it was said that it was Major Ropner who decided when the Baltic waters were open after the winter ice block, and his steamers were invariably the first available to load the cargoes of timber when navigation again became possible.

One winter *Seaton* was frozen in the Baltic for six weeks. The story goes that the captain, Ben Granger, had the ship's sides chipped down and then had one side painted grey and the other side black. The grey wore better and so for many years Ropner ships were painted that colour. The house flag they flew had the red and white checks of the International Code signal letter 'U', though Robert obviously chose it because it was also the town flag of Magdeburg where his father had been stationed when Robert was growing up. It has been better known to generations of seamen as 'the old bread and jam'.

So good was Robert's ability to obtain cargoes to and from the Baltic that sometimes he was obliged to charter ships belonging to Isaac Beddington to cover the amount of cargo he had procured for shipment. The necessity for this must have ceased by the end of the decade, however, for by then he had built up the biggest fleet of steamers in West Hartlepool with the addition of *Hesleden* in 1876, *Horden* and *Helmstedt* in 1877, *Crimdon* and *Elpis* in 1878, *Harlsey* and *Eden* in 1879 and *Parklands*, *Blackhalls*, the second *Hardwick* and the second *Lufra* in 1880. At 2010 gross tons *Elpis* was the largest vessel registered in the Hartlepools, a trend that Ropners have always tended to follow, as will be seen.

Besides increasing his fleet Robert considered expanding by opening offices in London and Cardiff, and in 1879 there is correspondence about the advisability of doing this with interested parties. Eventually he decided against opening an office in London but wrote in June that 'there is little doubt that the bulk of the overseas boat trade will in future be done from So. Wales and my steamers will more frequently load there.' He therefore took up the suggestion of a Mr J. Hoffman, who already had an office in Cardiff, that he should become the branch manager of R. Ropner & Co. there. 'You agree to act as my manager there,' Ropner wrote on 1 July, 'the firm to be the same as here, R. Ropner & Co., and you're to discontinue your own business and to give your whole time to me. Your salary to be £300, first year, £350, second year, £400, third year, £450, fourth year, £500, fifth year.' To this was later added 10 per cent of the branch's nett profits.

At some point in 1879 Robert also took on another clerk, a man called Lancaster, at 35s a week. Lancaster served the company even longer than Thwaites and was still to be seen before the Second World War on his tall stool in the Mainsforth Terrace offices in West Hartlepool, making up the voyage accounts which dominated the lives of all who first entered Ropners in the 1920s and 1930s. He must have been well into his eighties then and several senior members of the firm still working recall him well.

The indications are, however, that by the end of the year business had slumped and that Robert was faced with his first serious decline in trade. Early in 1880 he was writing to Hoffmann, who was proving unsatisfactory ('you have not only acted without my authority but in opposition to same'), that 'we have not earned anything these last few months and the prospects are wretched', and in May he took the decision to end his arrangement with him. 'I have come to the conclusion,' he wrote, 'that it will be best to discontinue the business there as I find we are not supported as I expected we should have been and it does not suit me to go about here begging for business. If you decide to go on in your name I shall be glad to support you.'

Begging for business was not Robert's way, but that did not mean he was above looking out for new trade to keep his fleet at sea. He wrote to a Mr Walter Scott at Newcastle the same month:

I notice that you have become the purchaser of the East Hetton and Frimdon Grange collieries, and should you require an agent for the sale of your coals I should be glad to act for you. Having represented the Haswell and Shotton Coal Co. for the last 20 years I of course thoroughly understand the coal trade and if appointed would be willing to guarantee the payment of all sales of your coals made by my firm. I have a fleet of 14 steamers and am therefore in an excellent position to influence the business; the coal trade is now mainly done by steamers and to have these at your command is a very great assistance in procuring trade.

Business, however, did not improve and in June 1880 he was obliged to write to an employee: 'I regret that the boat trade is so extremely bad that I am compelled to reduce the expenses', and mentions that the little trade he is doing is with Germany.

The adverse economic climate also called for sterner administration and on the same day Robert wrote to the captain of *Renpor* with dry humour that 'I regret to say that I am not quite satisfied with you. The *Renpor* never moves but she either receives or does damage, and it seems a continuation of claims, besides the passages you are making, are anything but satisfactory. I very much fear that I have promoted you too quickly.'

Despite such temporary setbacks there is little doubt that even after a few years on his own Robert had become a wealthy man. If confirmation of this is needed it is to be found in his correspondence over his purchase of the magnificent estate of Preston Hall (now a museum) on the outskirts of Stockton. After protracted negotiations the price of £27,500 for the house and 117 acres was agreed on 3 February 1881, but extensive refurbishment delayed him moving until 1 October 1882.

Preston Hall was the ideal surroundings for the young shipping magnate now in the prime of life. Many men would have been justified in feeling they had accomplished enough and turn their energies to pursuing the pleasures of life like good wine and hard hunting, and idling the summer away playing the newfangled game of lawn tennis. Robert did indeed enjoy all these pleasures – and passed them on to the present generation; his great-grandson, John, formerly Joint Master of the Bedale and the firm shares a Californian winery. He rode regularly to hounds until two accidents put an end to this pursuit, noted in July 1880 that the family were playing tennis 'almost daily', and the same year wrote to his wine merchants that he had tasted the Médoc and Sauternes sent to him for his approval. 'The former is rather sweet but will do but the latter is not at all like your former wine. It is as sweet as molasses and we cannot drink it.'

But one can assume that Robert's career in his own mind had only just begun. He enjoyed the good things of life but they did not distract him from his ultimate ambitions. Those first years on his own had merely been a consolidation of past hard work. On this solid base of commercial success he now began not only to build up an enterprise that became one of the largest tramp steamer companies in the country – and therefore the world – but to start carving out a career for himself as a politician and a philanthropist. Before proceeding further, however, it would be as well to describe in greater detail the nature of the business he was building up and the context in which he traded.

All the signs of the prosperity that was to give Britain such unprecedented economic expansion were present by the middle of the nineteenth century. Between 1801 and 1851 the population doubled, and it almost doubled again between 1851 and 1901 despite wholesale emigration which in itself was a great stimulus to commercial shipping. These huge rises in the population altered the balance of the country's economy; from being agriculturally self-sufficient Britain became a large exporter of the products of the industrial revolution and of coal in order to pay for food and the raw materials that had by then been mined out of her own soil. It has been calculated that between 1854 and 1874 the total value of imports into Britain rose by 143 per cent, while the total value of imported foodstuffs rose by 165 per cent over the same period. Between 1840 and 1887 one statistician calculated there was a sevenfold increase in maritime commerce.

All this vast increase in trade had to be moved by sea. By 1850 Britain owned 3.4 million of the 6.9 million tons of sailing ships in existence, but she was also at the forefront of developing the iron steamship, a vessel created by the pressure for larger, faster and more reliable bulk carriers to ply not only in British waters and to and from the Continent but to the newer markets of Australia, the United States and South America.

The iron, and later the steel, steamship did not supersede the sailing ship immediately; indeed, it was a drawnout process and they co-existed during most of the latter part of the century. But slowly the superiority of the steamship became more and more apparent, and eventually the invention of the triple expansion engine in the early 1880s enabled the newer vessel to operate with an economy and reliability the sailing ship could not equal. Once the steamer became established bunkering stations were needed world wide and it was Britain with her high thermal output coal that kept these stations supplied.

It was during this time of expansion and change that Robert Ropner was building up his fleet of steamers and expanding his trade far beyond British waters and the Baltic. After his first tiny cargo carrier, *Amy*, with her simple 80-h.p. engines, the Ropner ships were always fitted with two-cylinder compound engines which were continually being refined and improved. Higher boiler pressures and piston speeds led to fuel economy, and to lighter engines which also required less space. This in turn had a significant effect on profits, one contemporary commentator calculating that every ton of deadweight capacity was worth on average £10 a year in freight, so that saving a hundred tons with a lighter engine was worth an extra income of £1000 to the owners.

The compound engine was used in all Robert's ships until 1885 when *Greystoke* was fitted with the new three-cylinder triple expansion engine which reduced coal consumption still further. In 1891 it was estimated that with the use of the triple expansion engine fuel economy had improved 20 per cent compared with ten years previously.

The biggest advances in the design of Ropner ships were reserved until Robert went into shipbuilding himself, but there is little doubt that he ensured his steamers were the most modern available and were maintained and run in the most efficient and economical manner possible. This in turn meant that there was never any shortage of businessmen eager to take up a share in his steamers.

The economic and technical changes that took place during the last part of the nineteenth century had their influence on the manner in which Robert and similar shipowners traded. Appleby, Ropner had been coal exporters, finding markets in the British Isles and the Continent for the abundant high-quality coal produced by the northeast coalfields. When they started to own steamers they exported the coal in them and probably returned with pit props or other simple cargoes. During his first years on his own Robert must have made money where he could – as an agent for the local collieries, an exporter of coal and an importer of timber, as a ship's agent for visiting steamers from other fleets, and, increasingly, as someone who could manage steamers both efficiently and economically so that charterers knew they were getting their money's worth.

Tramping, that is being available on the open market to carry a cargo between any port at any time at the going rate, would have been at a very rudimentary stage, although, as has been mentioned, Robert had an uncanny knack of having his ships in just the right spot when a cargo needed to be shipped. But as the nation's economy expanded, and the steamers and trade, as well as communications like the telegraph and telephone, became more sophisticated, so the business of running a tramp fleet became a more specialized affair. Hence the need for branch offices in London – opened in 1887 – and Cardiff, for it was from these prime market places that charters were 'fixed', cargoes sought and freight rates established. R. Ropner & Co. may have been primarily merchants in 1875, but by 1895 they were shipowners.

The boom in shipping during the 1870s brought with it, almost inevitably, its own hazards, for speculators built tonnage to reap the rewards of the expansion in trade only to find the market flooded with steamers and the freight rates plunging. Between 1880 and 1885, for instance, British steamer tonnage went up from 2,949,282 nett tons to 4,308,643, and this massive increase inevitably led to the slump of 1884–85, the first really big downturn in trade since the introduction of the steamer. Never has the law of supply and demand worked so savagely as it does in the shipping market, and it was in those early years that Robert must have learned how to ride the bad patches by conserving his profits when freight rates soared. He must have learned too, as others did, the advantage of building new tonnage when the market was depressed, thereby obtaining the cheapest price, the best workmanship and prompt delivery dates. The skill was to judge the market accurately enough to know exactly when to build. But Robert was an expert at calculating the ideal moment for whatever he did. After all, if ever there was the right man in the right place at the right time, it was he.

3

Shipowner, Politician and Philanthropist

WITH fourteen steamers to find work for and a temporary downturn in trade, Robert paused for two years in the expansion of his fleet. But in 1882 he recommenced construction by ordering *Wellfield* and *Hartburn* from Ernest Withy's Middleton yard and *Watlington* and *Preston* from Wm Gray, the latter disappearing in March 1885 whilst on passage from New York to Avonmouth. Next came the second *Renpor* and *Gledholt*, both from Ernest Withy, before the severe recession in trade during 1884–85 stopped any more construction until 1885, when *Greystoke* and the second *Preston* were delivered, the first from Ernest Withy, the second from Matthew Pearse's yard at Stockton.

But Robert's expansion was not confined to building new steamers, for in June 1885 an agreement was drawn up between Robert and a Robert Morton Middleton Jr in which Robert agreed to buy shares in three steamers – *Alicia*, *Romanby* and *Sowerby* – up to the amount of £3000 and to take over their management. On 11 December Robert wrote to William Gray asking him to value the shares in these three steamers and from this letter it is obvious that Robert is taking on quite a financial burden:

You will observe that the prices have to be fixed at their 'fair market value' which, of course, is an entirely different thing to buying them as a going concern in order to obtain the management. In valuing the shares no allowance has been made for goodwill, as under the agreement Mr Middleton continues to share in the profits from the management. The date of transfer will be 1 January and the back averages for which I have to have allowances are very heavy, the steamers being heavily insured, viz:

Romanby £18,000, *Alicia* £14,000, and *Sowerby* £12,000.

It is therefore much to his credit that just over a year later he was able to say that the position of the three steamers was now thoroughly sound. *Romanby* would pay £10 per share for the first half of the year and *Alicia* £5, and all their accumulated debts had been paid off, as well as the very large amounts of back averages. They were now insured at Lloyds on a sound basis and Robert expected they would provide fair dividends in the future. The smallest ship, *Sowerby*, 'has still some leeway to make up', but her debts and her back averages had been paid off, as had her fee for her eight-year Lloyds survey, 'always a costly business'. 'We flatter ourselves,' he wrote to one shareholder, 'that we have done exceedingly well in pulling these boats thro' unprecedented times, in the position they were, without having to make a "call".'

The shareholders were obviously impressed and, despite some infighting with Middleton's brother, supported Robert's acquisition of a majority shareholding in the ships in 1887 when he became the owner of all three. However, in 1899, when a shareholder in *Romanby* wished to dispose of his interest in her, Robert revealed that all had not gone as smoothly as he would have wished. 'The *Romanby*,' he told the shareholder, 'is the worst steamer with which we have ever been connected and we have many times regretted that we took her over from Mr Middleton and she was, and is, a most unsatisfactory property. Had we known the trouble it would have entailed we would certainly never have had anything to do with any of the Middleton ships.'

It was, incidentally, almost certainly *Romanby* that started the long Ropner tradition – still observed – of naming their ships after northeastern villages whose names ended in 'by'. The fourth *Romanby* was launched in 1957.

Robert bought the shares for £70 each and then promptly sold the ship to a Norwegian owner. He always drove a hard bargain, but a fair one, and time and again his correspondence shows that, although he was a hardened negotiator who thoroughly disliked the notion that he might be being conned, he was a humane employer and a sympathetic friend. 'It does not do to make any difference in the wages of captains of similar ships and in the same trade,' he began a letter to the captain of *Wellfield* in February 1885 who had asked for a rise. Then, typically, having struck the right note of firmness, he softens and gives the captain a £2 bonus, ending the letter, 'Hoping you will do your best for *Wellfield* and that you will make a good voyage.' When some years later he was asked for a loan by a neighbour he wrote back: 'I have had very sad experiences in lending money and have always lost my money and a friend into the bargain. For this reason I made it a principle years ago not to again lend money.' Anyone reading this would have thought that the end of the matter. But not with Robert – he *gave* the man £3 3s od.

In 1887 Robert also added his first steel-hulled steamers to his fleet, *Picton*, built by Ernest Withy, and the second *Wave*, constructed at William Gray's yard. The same year he must have come to the conclusion that he could not avoid opening a London branch office any longer, and he came, it seems, to a similar arrangement with a Mr F. W. Elcomb to run one for him as he had with Hoffman in Cardiff eight years previously. Unlike the Cardiff arrangement, Elcomb worked out well and stayed the length of his ten-year contract after which it was decided to control the London operation direct from West Hartlepool. By 1903, when the Baltic Exchange opened its new building in St Mary Axe, Robert had already made arrangements for the branch office to move right next door. Where communication between the marketplace and the decision makers was essential, this proved an astute move indeed.

Between September 1880, when it had been closed down, and the beginning of 1886, there is no mention of the Cardiff office in correspondence. These were difficult trading years and it could be that it remained shut for some of them, but by January 1886 Robert was writing to his third son, William, there.

Dear Willie,
I have yours of yesterday with I O U for £208-12s-6d balance of your share in the *Preston* and hope you will soon save sufficient money to pay it off. The reports from her are good and I hope she will pay well. For regularity's sake I confirm that your salary this year will be a minimum £200, you having 1/6th of the nett profit should this exceed £200 and which I have no doubt it will if you work hard.

It is signed, as it always was to any of his children, 'your affectionate father'.

From this letter one can deduce that William had already been with the firm in 1885, when he had turned twenty-one. He could not have joined much before that as he had been sent abroad, probably to Germany, to learn the language, after finishing his education at Durham School. He almost certainly remained in Cardiff until his father began relinquishing the day-to-day running of the shipping side of his business during the 1890s, by which time a manager, D. M. Jones, had been appointed on a ten-year contract with a rising share of the profits.

William was gentle, quietly spoken and, like his father, impeccably dressed. Although he might not have had Robert's cutting edge in business, he had a tougher side – he played rugby for Cardiff and was a good all-round athlete. In the fullness of time the responsibilities of running the enterprise his father had created was to devolve on him, and his time in Cardiff, although it did not always agree with his health, must have been invaluable to him in later life.

Besides acquiring a major shareholding in three steamers, constructing his first steel-hulled ones, and taking the major step of opening a London branch office, Robert began in 1887 to buy shares in other people's ships in order to build up the chartering and brokerage side of his business. In November 1887 he is writing to a West Hartlepool shipowner that

> we agree to take 3/64th shares in your new steel steamer building by Messrs Wm Gray and Co. at the cost price on the terms mentioned in your letter but including the Newport chartering which as you are aware is nearly all done at Cardiff, the Newport charterers all having offices at Cardiff. It must also be understood that you will only accept a charter or buy bunkers through another source after our Cardiff people have failed to secure similar terms as offered you elsewhere which is most unlikely to happen. We hope that after you find how well this arrangement will work at Cardiff you will see your way to extend it to London also.

The same month Robert's eldest son, John, who had been made a partner the previous year, wrote to another shipowner that, having talked over the matter with his father, 'we would be disposed to take 12 shares in your new steamer at cost price in consideration of your giving us the chartering of your six steamers in London and South Wales.'

At the behest of Messrs Coverdale and Sons, West Hartlepool, Robert agreed in January 1888 to take on a Mr Sanderson at the Cardiff office

on the understanding that as long as Mr Sanderson remains with us, you give us in Cardiff the chartering and clearances of all the steamers managed by your goodselves which may go to Cardiff with the exception of one or two fixtures in a year, we agreeing to do your business on usual terms, say 1/6d (per ton) for brokering, £3-3s-od clearances fee for boats above 2000 tons cargo, £2-2s-od for boats less than this size and returning you the 3d fittage on bunkers in all cases when we receive same.

The following month Robert wrote to another local shipowner that he agreed to take 4/64ths share in S S *Paola* at £135 per 1/64th share provided

you put all homeward chartering of your steamers *Clematis*, *Bedlington*, and *Paola* in the hands of our London firm, at a remuneration to them of 1/5th of 5% brokerage on all Black Sea, Azoff, Danube, Mediterranean ore, and American charters, and 1/4th of 5% on all charters, this to be clear of whatever share of brokerage the charterers, or other brokers, may take, you to have the liberty of chartering timber from the Baltic direct with French brokers, but crediting us with any difference between the amount you pay for brokerage in France, and 1/4th of 5%.

These letters not only show Robert's acumen at picking up business by wise investment but reveal the kind of trade he was now engaged in and the terms on which he plied it. Having the capital, he used it cleverly, just as eighteen years before William Gray had cleverly used his when buying shares in Robert's first steamer by insisting he also take a percentage of the ship's management fees on top of his share of *Lufra*'s profits.

The impression one gets from this and other correspondence is that the years 1887–88 were ones in which Robert took the final steps in securing the future of his enterprise by putting it on such a solidly successful foundation that it has remained unshaken through two world wars and a number of severe economic depressions.

By the beginning of 1887 the market had begun to improve again and the fact that Robert now had a fleet of modern steamers, which included a number of the larger, well-deck types, enabled him to take full advantage of the higher freight rates. In turn this spurred him on to order four more well-deck ships, *Elton*, *Crathorne*, *Hurworth* and *Swainby*, from William Gray for delivery in 1888.

As his fleet and his success grew, Robert was never short of people to take shares in his steamers. They clamoured for them. At times it must have been embarrassing. 'We had to close our lists for the November/December and February/March boats within 2 days of writing to our friends,' he wrote in the middle of 1888 to a potential investor, and the year before he had informed another that 'I am not offering the shares in my new steamer to anyone outside my circle of friends . . . I shall keep at least half of the boat myself.' Nevertheless, he often relented and sold shares to close friends when he would have preferred to keep them himself. He also saw to it that his sons used their income properly. 'In order to get your money employed again as soon as possible,' he wrote to William at the end of 1887, 'I will sell you a share in a new steel boat (*Elton*) expected ready about the end of the month.' If necessary he advanced them the money to buy shares in his ships – but it was always done on a businesslike basis.

In 1888 he also took the logical step of buying a shipyard himself. Doubtless, his motivation was the same as it had been when he had bought *Amy* twenty years previously, but he probably also wanted to ensure suitable employment for his other sons. In the course of time both Robert Jr and Leonard joined the shipyard side of the business, while Walter, the youngest, went to work in the London office.

Initially, Robert had apparently cast around in West Hartlepool for a suitable shipyard but was unable to purchase one. Instead, he looked in Stockton, a town in which he was taking an increasing interest, and finally purchased the yard of Matthew Pearse & Co., which had built the second *Preston* for him in 1885. 'It is my intention,' he wrote to the yard's auditors, 'to carry on Messrs Pearse's yard at Stockton, but in a very quiet way, and I do not expect any great results for some time.'

Robert was always prone to understatement. The pragmatic, cautious approach is the hallmark of his correspondence, but it is hard to believe that on this occasion he entirely believed what he had written. Certainly, it bears no relation to what actually transpired, as by the end of the following year the yard had already produced four more steamers for him, *Maltby*, *Thornaby*, *Aislaby* and *Raisby*, and then went on to deliver to him nearly sixty more before the outbreak of the First World War. It also built a lot of tonnage for other owners, including a Captain W. Smith who, with Robert's encouragement, founded the well-known South Wales shipping firm of William Reardon Smith and Sons Ltd. So successful was the yard that by 1895 it was the third largest in Britain and the following year had an output of 50,000 tons.

Owning the Stockton yard also gave Robert another lever with which to expand further his chartering and broking business, and before long we find him writing to some local shipowners confirming their order for a steel steamer. He gave them generous payment terms and also agreed to buy 8/64ths in another new steamer they were having built on the Tyne. In return he stipulated they 'give to my firms the whole of the chartering of this steamer, and also of the steamer I have sold you today, in all trades and to and from all ports, my firm's remuneration to be 1/3rd of the usual 5% brokerage on all charters.'

Underpinned by Robert's determination to make his branches successful, both the London and Cardiff offices flourished. In April 1889 he was able to write to Elcomb: 'I think you have done extremely well and quite expect the nett profits will reach £5000 pa within a couple of years.' Exactly a year later he wrote: 'I am very pleased to find that you have done so well in the cotton trade last year', and to William he confirmed that 'I agree with you that the result for last year is very satisfactory. We must hope that it may continue altho' I scarcely think so.'

Again Robert proved to be right, and by the end of 1890 freight rates had plunged, a situation which lasted for several years. By this time, however, Ropners was in a position to survive any downturn in trade and although various strikes in the coal and engineering businesses hindered recovery to some extent one gathers from correspondence that this was more a matter that caused irritation than any substantial financial losses.

During the 1890s one detects a subtle change in the tone of Robert's surviving correspondence. He was now approaching his sixties and, like many men of a similar age, he began to take a more detached view of life. 'As long as one is in business,' he wrote at the end of 1893, 'one is bound to go on or be out-stripped in the Race. I look upon our businesses as mere trifles in comparison with some big undertakings, but life is short and you cannot achieve all that you would wish.'

Though no definite dates are available it must have been during these last years of the century that Robert began to hand over the day-to-day running of the businesses to his sons, in order that he could pursue his other interests. In 1895, when he was still attending the office daily, he renewed his ten-year partnership contract with John – who continued to have a 4/20th share of the nett profits from the West Hartlepool, London and Cardiff offices – and shortly afterwards extended William's partnership for another five years. Certainly by 1903 the handover had been completed, for in July of that year he wrote to a member of the Cardiff staff that he took 'no interest in the management of the steamers now'.

A larger percentage of his letters were now concerned with local politics, for as he withdrew from the running of his businesses so he began to occupy himself more with the affairs of Stockton and with the wider interests of the shipping industry. In 1889 he became a county councillor for the southwest ward of Stockton and the same year was appointed justice of the peace for the County of Durham. In 1890 he gave the borough of Stockton 36 acres of land for a public park and the following year was made the town's first freeman. At a dinner in his honour he made a characteristic speech which was summarized by a local paper.

He was delighted to be made the first freeman of the ancient borough of Stockton – (applause) – but if it had not been accompanied, as it was that night, by their (the company's) cordial expression of goodwishes, he was afraid he should not have thought so much of it, and he must plead guilty to thinking as much of their kindness in entertaining him that night as he did of the freedom of the borough. (Applause) After all, life was short and appeared but a dream; and unless they were supported in some measure by the good words and wishes of their fellow townsmen, it was scarcely worth while to live at all. (Hear, hear) With regard to his gift (of the park), he was very much afraid they were making far too much of it. (No, no) He himself had the best part of the bargain by a long way. (Laughter) Surely the pleasure he derived from having given that ground was very much greater – (loud applause) – it must be ten thousand times greater than the pleasure they could possibly have in receiving the land.

From this time Robert's popularity in the town went from strength to strength and at the end of the following year he was made mayor for 1893. In 1894 he became a member of the Tees Conservancy Commission, a post he held until 1920. Two years later he became Deputy Lieutenant for the County of Durham and was also High Sheriff that year. Already a member of the Hartlepool Port and Harbour Commission since 1889, he became its chairman in 1898, a post he held until 1901. The same year he became chairman of the Hartlepools Shipping Federation and continued in this capacity until 1915. In 1899 he became a justice of the peace for the North Riding of Yorkshire. In addition to these commitments, he was a director of many public companies, including several marine insurance firms, and in 1891 the Hartlepools Shipowners' Society had him elected to the General Committee of Lloyds' Register of Shipping, London, on which his great-grandson, David, sits. During these years he continued to give generously of his time and money to local charities and institutions. In 1897 he gave a convalescent home to the workmen of Stockton and Thornaby and later endowed the Stockton hospitals with a gift of £10,000.

But although still very much involved in his business as well as in local philanthropic works, Robert's main interest in the 1890s lay in his support of the Unionist cause and in the work of the Chamber of Shipping.

The Chamber of Shipping had been founded in 1878 to represent the interests of shipowners. No doubt Robert had been involved with it since its inception and by 1899, when he became a member of its executive council, it was an august body with considerable influence both in and outside Parliament. In 1900 Robert became its vice-president and in 1901 its president, a post he held for the unusually long period of two years.

In his inaugural speech as president Robert said:

I may, perhaps, claim to represent more especially the cargo carrying steamer, or 'cargo tramp' as it is often called, to distinguish it from the 'liner', and it is, I trust, with pardonable pride that I venture to point out the important position held in the shipping world by this class of vessel. It is sometimes overlooked that the 'cargo tramp' is, and always has been, the pioneer of the shipping trade. There is scarcely a port or harbour throughout the world the trade of which has not, in the first instance, been opened out by the 'cargo tramp', and as a rule it is only when the trade of a port or harbour has assumed considerable dimensions that the advent of the 'liner' is heralded. By far the greater bulk of the ocean carrying trade of the world is still done by the 'cargo tramp', and so long as the protection of a powerful Navy is available, the 'cargo tramp' will be able to carry the bulk of the enormous quantity of food-stuff necessary to feed our immense population without fear of a recurrence of the high prices ruling, for example, during the Crimean War.

Closely allied to Robert's work for the Chamber of Shipping was his interest in national politics which culminated in him entering Parliament in 1900, receiving a knighthood for his services to shipping in 1902 and being made a baronet in 1904.

In 1889 Robert had become chairman of the Stockton Conservative Party which successfully returned their candidate to Parliament that year. Correspondence shows that Lord Londonderry later urged Robert to fight for the Cleveland constituency during the 1895 election, and that at first Robert declined to do so. Eventually he relented although he knew he had little chance of winning – a complete forlorn hope as he called it. In fact, he came nearer to winning the seat than any previous Unionist, but was again defeated in 1898. However, by then he had proved himself as astute in politics as in business and when he was invited to fight the Stockton seat he won in a closely contested struggle. He made his maiden speech on 2 May 1901 when, despite his interest in keeping tax on coal low, he spoke in favour of a tax on exported coal imposed by the government to raise money for the Boer War. As an exporter of coal himself he was able to speak with authority on the subject. However, thereafter he was an untiring supporter of the shipping industry. *Hansard* records that he also spoke in debates on the Workers Compensation Act and in the debate on the Land Tenure Act, both of which must have been of considerable personal interest to him for he now owned the large estate of Skutterskelfe, at Hutton Rudby in Yorkshire, which he had bought in 1898.

Hansard records, too, that he was a keen supporter of the Act to abolish light dues – a subject in which David Ropner, as chairman of the Lights Advisory Committee, is also involved – and was a frequent speaker during the debates to amend the Merchant Shipping Acts. In 1906, the year he retained his Stockton seat, he spoke no less than twenty-two times, and he continued to serve his constituents for another four years before retiring, aged seventy-one, in 1910.

For a foreign teenage stowaway, Sir Robert Ropner Bt, VD, JP, MP, had come a lot further than even he might have envisaged during that rough passage across the North Sea over half a century previously.

4
Peace and War

WITH their father increasingly involved in politics and the Chamber of Shipping, it devolved upon John and William to steer the shipping side of the business through the ups and down in trade that preceded the First World War. By all accounts they were exceedingly good at it. The first really severe slump in the mid-1890s – *The Shipping World* called 1894 'one of the poorest experienced', while the following September a writer in the magazine announced that 'never in the history of steam shipping have coal freights touched such a level of depression as they have this summer' – no doubt gave the brothers a foretaste of what was to come. But in no sense did it hinder the steady expansion of the Ropner fleet. By May 1894 it possessed thirty-five steamers with a combined gross registered tonnage of 77,750, with two more steamers under construction. And in the two years between 1895 and 1897 nine new vessels were delivered by the Stockton yard, including the first trunk-deck steamer, *Trunkby*.

This revolutionary new design, patented by Robert Jr, had a steel trunk built on the main deck for practically the whole length of the ship. This improved stability when loaded, gave greater cargo capacity and protected the hatches – always a vulnerable point – from the seas that broke over a ship in heavy weather. Probably inspired by the American whaleback steamer – one of which visited the U K in 1892 causing much interest amongst marine architects – many of these vessels were built by the Stockton yard for Ropners.

They proved most satisfactory for carrying homogeneous bulk cargoes, although less so for general cargoes due to the absence of 'tween decks. However, they were primarily built because the Suez Canal Authority regulations exempted the trunkspace from their tonnage measurements and this made them cheaper to run to the Far East and Australia than the conventional steamer as their canal dues were less. An improved version appeared in 1907, but this form of design was eventually discontinued as it was found that when in ballast the steamers had a rather high centre of gravity which impaired their stability.

At the turn of the century the first short-bridge vessels of around 6000 tons deadweight began to be built. These were economical if slow ships used for the Black Sea, Danube and River Plate trades. Built at around £5 per ton, they proved to be highly profitable.

In 1911 the Stockton yard delivered its first prototype long-bridge-type vessel, the 8750-ton dw steamer *Levenpool*, to Ropners. These ships were developed to overcome the necessity for greater cargo space without increasing the vessel's draft. Length was the cheapest method of increasing capacity, but when this was done by some designers at the expense of draft it proved dangerous. Lloyds' Register of Shipping therefore placed a limit of 12 on the length:depth ratio of a steamer. However, if the ship possessed a full-height, continuous superstructure covering at least 70 per cent of the length amidships, the length:depth ratio was allowed to be increased to 14. This made long-bridge ships an attractive proposition, for their type of construction increased their carrying capacity without increasing their nett registered tonnage. This not only cut the cost of canal dues but also port and light dues, and towage and pilotage charges, which, under British rules, were also calculated by a vessel's nett tonnage. An added benefit of the long-bridge design was that latitudinal bunker spaces could be built across the width of the ship. Known as cross-bunkers, these were big enough to hold sufficient fuel for long passages to obviate the need for expensive refuelling en route.

Not unnaturally the long-bridge ships were used on the longer trade routes, like the nitrate run to the west coast of South America, but they did not entirely supersede the smaller short-bridge steamers which continued to be the backbone of the fleet up to the First World War. However, the long-bridge steamers were themselves superseded in due course by the shelter-decker. It did so because it exploited even more efficiently than the long-bridge type the rule governing the calculation of nett tonnage whereby any space not totally enclosed could be deducted from the gross tonnage. It had two decks and in appearance a continuous upper deck. But in fact there was what was called a tonnage opening in the after part of the 'tween deck which was only temporarily closed, so the whole of that 'tween deck could be deducted from the vessel's gross tonnage.

Once the Stockton yard took over the responsibility of supplying the new tonnage, and the newer types of steamer began to be introduced, losses dropped dramatically. Only three of the ships built between 1896 and 1914 were lost between these dates, one of them in a collision; and this at a time when the fleet was steadily increasing each year. By comparison, nineteen had been lost or abandoned up to the turn of the century and four more of the older type up to the First World War. These statistics would probably have been worse if between 1898 and 1900 fourteen of the older steamers had not been sold off, giving Robert the liquidity to invest heavily in stocks, which correspondence shows he did around this time.

By the early 1900s both John and William were well-established businessmen and public figures in their own right. Both were married – John in 1888 to Margaret MacGregor and William in 1894 to Sarah Wollacott Cory – but whereas William had four sons and a daughter – Leonard (1895), William Guy (1896), John Raymond (1903), Robert Desmond (1908) and Constance Winsome (1899) – John had two daughters. With no male heir, the baronetcy John inherited from his father in 1925 passed on his death in 1936 to Robert Jr's son, also called Robert, a branch of the family which does not have any direct interest in Ropners today.

Doubtless, the fact that John had no male heirs affected the brothers' attitude to running the shipping side of the business. Those alive now remember John as someone who, after the First World War, only came into the office occasionally. If the firm required a bridging loan – and in those bleak days it sometimes did – he was always ready to oblige at a favourable rate, but he left the day-to-day running of the business to William and his sons.

In the early years of the century, however, John was doubtless as active as William in the business. Like his father, he became in due course High Sheriff for the County of Durham and its Deputy

Lieutenant. He also followed his father into the Volunteer force and finished his military career as honorary colonel of 1st Volunteer Battalion, the Durham Light Infantry, and earned the Volunteer Decoration. He was, too, a justice of the peace for the Hartlepool division of the County of Durham.

William was a JP, as well, but otherwise took up his father's other interests. In 1895 he fought in the Durham County bye-election and won the seat for the northwest division of West Hartlepool by fifty-three votes, but his political career seems to have petered out after this. Later, he became chairman of the Hartlepool Port and Harbour Commission and was a great supporter of a number of charities, including the Crippled Children's League.

Though by 1903 Robert was no longer involved in the running of his businesses he nevertheless kept a close eye on what was going on, and in September 1902 we find him writing to the owners of *Therese Heymann*, in which he had shares, saying that he was sorry to see from the balance sheet that the ship was so much in debt, and advised selling her, 'especially as the prospects at the moment are not encouraging'. However, he would not bind himself to putting his proportion of the shares into another boat. In fact, in May 1903 the owners wisely decided to put the steamer under Ropner management. Presumably she traded profitably from then on as she stayed with the firm until she disappeared in December 1914, having probably struck a mine.

The same year it was decided that another shipping company should be created, one that did not involve the sixty-fourths method of ownership. The Pool Shipping Company, a limited company, was formed to acquire and wholly own steamers – though these were still to be managed by R. Ropner & Co. The company was floated with a nominal capital of £25,000. It did so well with about half issued that, after the firm had called up the remainder of the capital in 1912, the nominal capital was increased in 1914 to £500,000 when a further issue of £125,000 was quickly taken up by shareholders. In 1919 the shareholders received a one-for-three bonus and a one-for-four bonus in 1920 when the capital was further increased, eventually reaching £937,500.

The company acquired its first ships the same year when the Stockton yard delivered *Heronspool* and *Troutpool*, and from that time all the company's ships had the suffix 'pool'. At the outbreak of war it had fourteen. Dividends of between 5 and 7 per cent were paid for the first four years, a good return when it is known that the average dividend paid by industry at that time was under 4 per cent.

Between 1907 and 1908, and again between 1910 and 1911, there was a severe slump in shipping which coincided with the highest rates of unemployment recorded during the first two decades of the century. The fall in the price of coal and legislation like the Merchant Shipping Amendment Act and the Workmen's Compensation Act contributed, in the opinion of many shipowners, to this sharp downturn in trade. Certainly, raising the loadline by 10½ inches, which came into force in 1906, increased available tonnage by 1 million tons at a stroke and this in itself must have further destabilized an already unsteady freight market.

The slump hit the small shipowners especially badly, and in 1908 J. A. Wood & Co. of West Hartlepool sold *Teesdale* to Ropners, and the following year Leask, Clark & Co., also of West Hartlepool, sold them *Martin*. By buying at the bottom of the market John and William were using their father's successful tactics, for in due course the market recovered and both ships traded successfully. By the end of 1911 profits and dividends in the Pool Shipping Co. surpassed their previous peak and continued to rise until 1913 when a dividend of 25 per cent was declared.

In January 1914 *Saxilby* was delivered by the Stockton yard, bringing the total number of steamers in both companies to fifty-seven. With the exception of *Swainby*, built in 1917, *Saxilby* was to be the last ship built for Ropners until 1918, and the intervening years were as tragic for the firm as it was for the rest of the civilized world.

The record of Ropner ships sunk in the First World War is a long and harrowing one, but from it can be gleaned something of the bravery during that time of the merchant service in general and Ropner seamen in particular. But, apart from *Hawnby*, stranded on 11 September 1914 because of the absence of shore lights, and *Selby*, sunk by a mine without loss of life on 30 September 1914, Ropners' first taste of war came not at sea but on land.

At eight o'clock in the morning, on 16 December 1914, units of the German High Seas Fleet launched the first attack on mainland Britain since 1798 by bombarding the Hartlepools, Whitby and Scarborough. Included in the attacking force were three of the enemy's largest, fastest and most heavily armed battle cruisers, *Blücher*, *Moltke* and *Seidlitz*, and it was these three ships which concentrated on the Hartlepools. Casualties in the two towns were high, 128 people being killed and 400 injured. During the bombardment, which lasted about an hour, the offices of the firm in Mainsforth Terrace were hit. The damage, however, was not serious and no one was injured as none of the staff had started work. But a shell exploded in William Ropner's home, Ambleside, unfortunately killing the cook.

The Hartlepool battery, manned by two companies of local artillerymen including William's two eldest sons, Leonard and Guy, kept up heavy return fire, though their 6-inch guns were no match for the 11-inch armament of the German battle cruisers. But the battery registered many hits and kept the Germans so occupied that they failed to do any damage at all to the docks or the steelworks which were their primary targets. The commander of *Blücher* was captured later in the war after the Battle of the Dogger Bank and he was able to confirm that the battery had done considerable damage to the German ships.

As light relief, it should also be mentioned that it was later recorded that immediately the shelling started the Royal Garrison Artillery's mascot, an Airedale dog, went to Hartlepool station and took the first train inland, but there is no record of whether it was court-martialled.

On Christmas Day 1914 *Therese Heymann* left the Tyne with a cargo of coal bound for Savona and was never seen again. At around the same time it was reported that several steamers had been mined off Filey and it was assumed *Therese Heymann* must have been one of them.

The first direct contact a Ropner ship had with the enemy was on 20 February 1915 when *Willerby*, on the way from Marseilles to the River Plate, was sunk by the German raider, *Prinz Eitel Friedrich*, south of Cape Verde Islands. Captain Wedgwood, in command of *Willerby*, later reported that the German cruiser was almost upon the steamer before he saw her. The German signalled for Wedgwood to stop but the captain ignored the order, whereupon the cruiser swerved astern of her. Captain Wedgwood quickly ordered his engines astern, hoping to ram the German, but the cruiser escaped by a few yards. The steamer was sunk and the crew taken on board and later landed in the United States along with the crews of French and Russian merchant ships destroyed by the raider.

The sinking of *Willerby* took place in defiance of international law for she was unarmed and unescorted, and it took the British authorities more than two years to realize that the Germans considered anything flying an Allied, or even a neutral, flag a legitimate target. But at this stage of the war they were still showing a degree of humanity and courtesy, and Captain Wedgwood was even furnished with a receipt for his ship, which read:

Atlantic ocean, 6th March 1915, the English steamer *Willerby* was captured and declared a prize by auxiliary cruiser *Prince Eitel Friederick*, at 12.10 pm on 20 February 1915, and in the same day in 1°8′ and 29°14′ West Long. she was sunk. The crew were taken on board the auxiliary cruiser; they were given the opportunity to take with them their belongings. Signed: Captain Commandant.

The crew of *Coleby*, on passage from Rosario to Britain with a cargo of grain, was treated with equal courtesy when, on 27 March 1915, she was overhauled by the German raider *Kronprinz Wilhelm* and forced to heave to. Her captain, William Crighton, was then handed a written statement in German and English. The English text read as follows:

I hereby give you the official proklamation.

1. *Your ship is a hostile one.*
2. *The cargo of your ship are hostile goots and conterbande.*
3. *You must immedeastely go with all your crew on board of the auxiliary; personel goods can be taken along.*
4. *Resistance will result an compulsion.*

Atlantick, den 27 Marz 1915

The German captain's spelling might not have been too good, but the message was clear enough and the crew did as they were bid.

They were then taken to the United States and landed, and *Coleby*'s second engineer, a man named Girdwood who later became the firm's Tyne superintendent, later spoke very highly of the way the Germans treated the *Coleby*'s crew.

By then, however, this kind of behaviour had ceased around British waters, for on 4 February the German Government had declared that on and after 18 February all merchant shipping seen in waters around the British Isles would be sunk on sight without regard for the safety of either passengers or crew.

Four days after the German policy came into force *Oakby*, under the command of Captain F. J. Bartlett, left London in ballast for South Wales. On 24 February she was off Folkestone when she was struck in number one hold by a torpedo. She was only a small ship, just under 2000 tons, and the impact blew in the bulkheads and within five minutes her forecastle was beginning to go under. Water and escaping steam started to fill the engine room which had to be abandoned without closing down the engines. The propeller continued to turn and began to drive her down, making it impossible to launch the lifeboats. It was then that the second engineer, Stanley Robinson, volunteered to return to the engine room, for he knew, as they all must have done, that if the ship went down she would not just sink, she – and the crew – would probably be blown to pieces when the sea reached the furnaces. He managed to get below and find the wheel for the main steam and turn it off. The propeller stopped driving the ship forward and down and the lifeboats were launched. *Oakby* sunk almost as soon as they touched the water. Robinson was subsequently awarded the Bronze Medal for Gallantry in saving life at sea.

The ruthless sinking of civilian shipping without warning, and the consequent hardening of every Englishman's attitude to anyone or anything connected with Germany, evoked a strong response from Robert, and in May 1915, shortly after the sinking of *Lusitania*, he wrote from Preston Hall to *The Times*:

Sir, unfortunately I was born in Germany, but for nearly 60 years I have resided in this country, and I have been naturalized for 54 years. To all who know me an assurance of loyalty to my adopted country and King is, I think, unnecessary, but as it has been suggested that silence might be interpreted as 'sitting on the gate', I take this opportunity of publicly expressing my abhorrence and detestation of the barbarous methods of German warfare, and the sinking of passenger steamers, which cannot be described in other words than 'foul murder'.

The crew of the next ship to be torpedoed, *Gadsby* on 1 July 1915, escaped safely and landed on the Irish coast, but the crew of *Glenby* were early victims of the Germans' harsh new policy at sea. Under the command of Captain J. T. Frost, she left Cardiff on 16 August 1915 with a cargo of coal. The next day, while in the St George's Channel, she was fired on by what the captain later reported as being a very speedy submarine in the region of 230 feet long. The crew abandoned ship, but the submarine continued to fire on the helpless men as they escaped in the lifeboats, two of the men being killed and another two wounded. On the same day *Kirkby*, under Admiralty charter, was attacked and sunk by a submarine in the Bristol Channel, but Captain W. Hewison and his crew escaped safely, as did the crew of *Scawby* when she was sunk by a submarine in the Mediterranean on 6 October 1915 whilst under the command of Captain M. A. Fisker.

The final victim in 1915 was the long-bridge steamer *Levenpool*. Only four of the Pool Shipping Company's ships were lost in the First World War, against thirty-two of the 'managed' fleet, as the larger tonnage usually operated out of range of the U-boats, which caused a large percentage of the casualties. *Levenpool*, however, was carrying a general cargo from New York to Rotterdam for the Belgian Relief Committee when she was mined off the Kentish Knock on 16 December 1915. She was badly damaged but was kept afloat and beached the next day. Luckily, none of her crew was injured in the explosion. With great difficulty her cargo was unloaded, and on 29 April 1916 she was refloated after a temporary wooden shield had been fitted over the damage. She was then able to proceed under her own steam to the Tyne where permanent repairs were made, and by the end of July 1916 she was ready for sea again. She survived the rest of the war and served Ropners well until she was broken up in Scotland in 1934.

5
The Fleet Fights Back

THE first eighteen months of the war had depleted the Ropner fleet badly. But worse was to come, with the next three years bringing a steady increase in the U-boat warfare that so nearly strangled British supply lines. In 1916 two Ropner ships were sunk in this manner, while one was sent to the bottom by a raider, one by a mine, and a third was wrecked.

February 1916 proved to be the most disastrous month. On 13 February *Dromonby*, while under command of Captain J. Brockett and under Admiralty requisition, was captured and sunk in the Atlantic by the German raider, *Moewe*. The crew were taken aboard the raider and then transferred after a few days to a captured steamer called *Appam* which eventually landed them safely in the United States. Two days later, *Ashby*, under the command of Captain Samuel Green and also under Admiralty requisition, was driven ashore at Ushant during a severe gale, the captain and one seaman being drowned. Finally, on 28 February *Thornaby*, on passage from Marbella to the East Coast with Captain D. Evans in command, struck a mine off the Downs and sank with all hands with the exception of the steward, one fireman and the pilot, who were picked up by a passing steamer.

The next Ropner ship to be sunk was *Trunkby* on 27 May 1916. Under the command of Captain William Owens, she was under Admiralty requisition when she was attacked and sent to the bottom by an enemy submarine, though fortunately the entire crew was saved. Three days later another Ropner ship, *Salmonpool*, in ballast for the United States, was attacked and sunk by a submarine some miles off Tunis, where Captain J. E. Jones and his crew were safely landed.

In 1917 merchant ships at last began to be armed, but in January two more Ropner ships were sunk by enemy submarines. *Wragby* was sent to the bottom off Gibraltar – Captain J. C. Wilson and his crew were all saved – on 4 January, and ten days later *Martin*, under the command of Captain John White, was sunk in the Bay of Biscay whilst on passage from Batonne to the Bristol Channel with a cargo of pitwood. Again, the crew got safely away in the lifeboats and were picked up by a French patrol boat. However, the master of a third ship to be sunk in the early months of 1917 was not so lucky. *Burnaby* left Cardiff for the Mediterranean on 10 January 1917 with a cargo of coals when she was torpedoed and sunk off Gibraltar. None of the crew was hurt but Captain J. C. Wilson was taken prisoner and later sent to Austria where he remained until the end of the war. The firm sent him parcels of food and clothing without which, he said when he eventually returned, he could not have survived. While he was a prisoner Captain Wilson's wages were paid in full by the firm.

After years of being helpless victims of the U-boats' indiscriminate attacks the Ropner fleet now began to strike back. The phrase 'Ropner's Navy' did not become common coinage until the early days of the Second World War, but it had its beginnings in the dark days of 1917 when the U-boat menace reached its height, for one Ropner ship struck back at the enemy with a fierceness that must have taken the Germans by surprise.

April 1917 was the worst month of the tense struggle to keep open Britain's supply lines. In that month we lost 196 ships, half a million tons, our allies lost 108, and the various neutral countries lost 126. It was the month that made the Admiralty realize that the convoy system had to be introduced. This form of protecting merchantmen, plus improved methods of hunting submarines, eventually turned the tide. During 1914 and 1915 only twenty-four enemy submarines had been sunk. In 1916 twenty-five were sent to the bottom, way below the Germans' capacity for building them, but by 1917 methods of tracking and destroying them brought up the total to ten during the first three months alone, and this increased to twelve during the next quarter. And one of these was the victim of a Ropner ship.

Wandby, under the command of Captain David Simpson, was in convoy between Bilbao and Newport with a load of iron ore when her steering chains broke in the Bay of Biscay. She was forced to drop out of the convoy and by dawn the next morning, 2 April, a gale had sprung up which must have badly hampered the repair work. However, it was completed and the ship was doubtless at her full speed of a mere 8 knots to rejoin the convoy when the crew saw a flash and then the white splash of a shell bursting in the sea astern. 'There was no chance of running away,' wrote the master in his report afterwards, 'it was either a case of throwing up the sponge or fighting, and we pegged away at him.'

At first though they had nothing to peg away at with their solitary gun mounted on the ship's stern as the roughness of the sea hid the submarine from their view. After the U-boat's sixth shot, however, they spotted her and opened fire. The submarine was the latest type and mounted two 4-inch guns, one of which was firing shrapnel. Soon the sides and decks of *Wandby* were scarred with it, while the heavier shells began to drop nearer and nearer until eventually one of them struck the port quarter and exploded just above the waterline. In all the submarine fired thirty-six shells at the *Wandby* from its position two miles astern of her, and one man was badly wounded. The rate of *Wandby*'s gun on her poop was very much slower for to train the weapon in such heavy seas must have been extremely difficult. Nevertheless, her fifteenth shot struck home and, in the master's words, 'the last we saw of him was his bows up in the air, and he went down stern first.' The fight had lasted three quarters of an hour.

For this brave action and its outcome Captain Simpson and his crew were awarded sums of money by the Director of Transport and Shipping. The Shipping Federation also awarded their gold medal and diploma to the master, and three members of his crew, the first officer, W. W. J. Beaven, the fourth engineer, George Henry Blogg, and the chief gunner, Hugh Stag, with their silver medal and diploma. At the conclusion of the war Captain Simpson was decorated with the O B E for his services and in October 1919 Lloyds honoured him when the chairman of the Liverpool Underwriters' Association, Mr J. Sandeman Allen, presented him with Lloyds' silver medal for meritorious service. 'I congratulate you on your courage,' Mr Allen said as he pinned the medal on *Wandby*'s master, 'and thank you, on behalf of the shipping community, as representing one of those gallant fellows of the Mercantile Marine, who has done so much for us.'

Captain Simpson was obviously one of those bluff old seadogs who had just done what had to be done. He had been with Ropners since 1899, when he had joined *Tenby* as third mate, and had been a master in the firm since 1906 when he had been given command of *Ormesby*. 'Making a speech is not my line,' he said on receiving the medal. 'We have not done any more than others have done, but we are one of the lucky ones and came out on top.'

Another Ropner master to be recognized for his bravery was Captain T. M. Hill who had what must have been one of the most extraordinary records of any Merchant Navy officer in either war.

Thirlby had been caught at Cronstadt when war was declared. She stayed there two years until the firm managed to get her out of the Baltic. However, this proved to be such an expensive operation for the firm that the government agreed she should be run free of requisition until the end of the war. Unfortunately for the firm, they did not benefit by this arrangement for long. On 24 April 1917, whilst under the command of Captain Hill, she was on passage from Bombay to Dunkirk without the protection of a convoy. At 0730 the track of a torpedo was suddenly seen crossing the ship's bows. The crew waited for the U-boat to attack again and the ship's short-range 12-pounder Vickers gun was manned. For forty minutes nothing happened, but the crew continued on the alert and at 0810 the wake of a second torpedo was sighted. Captain Hill, however, was able to swing his ship away from the track and the torpedo passed harmlessly astern. Ten minutes passed and then the submarine fired a third torpedo, but again it was seen in time for the master to alter course. Four minutes later the submarine surfaced right astern. As it rose out of the water the gun on *Thirlby*'s poop opened fire and the U-boat promptly dived out of sight only to re-emerge again three miles astern, beyond the effective range of the ship's weapon. From that distance the submarine began to shell *Thirlby* methodically. Whenever it crept closer *Thirlby* returned its fire while Captain Hill took desperate evasive action. The submarine kept up its steady fire from its two guns and after its hundredth or so shot managed to find its target. The shell hit one of *Thirlby*'s hatches and exploded amongst the cargo, doing little damage. Encouraged, the submarine closed with *Thirlby*, but was again driven off by her solitary gun. It continued to fire, however, and by midday it had expended 150 shells without doing any further damage. In reply *Thirlby* fired fifty-seven shells, managing to get off about a dozen rounds in the first couple of minutes of the engagement. In the meantime all the crew, with the exception of the master, a seaman and the steward, who was helping the gunners, were below in the stokehold helping to get the greatest possible speed out of the steamer. For four and a half hours she manoeuvred and fought until one of her shells hit the submarine in the conning tower. It then broke off the action and disappeared astern just as another ship appeared on the horizon. This vessel had wireless and a signal was sent out for help, and within two hours a destroyer was alongside *Thirlby* obtaining the submarine's last known position.

For his part in the battle Captain Hill was subsequently awarded the Shipping Federation's gold medal and diploma. Three of his crew, the chief officer, E. W. Jackson, the steward, E. Wake, and one of the junior seamen, W. S. Sheriff, were awarded the silver medal and diploma.

On *Thirlby*'s next voyage, still under the command of Captain Hill, she was torpedoed 200 miles from the Irish coast on 2 July 1917. Loaded with ore as she was, she sank in a very short time. Two of the crew were killed and the rest took to the lifeboats. The submarine then came alongside and the Germans took away the lifeboats' sails. Despite this despicable act the crew were eventually rescued by a patrol boat and landed on the Irish coast.

After his safe return from Ireland Captain Hill was requested by the firm to take command of *Teesdale* which had been torpedoed and temporarily repaired. He was on passage to the Tees in her when, off Redcar, the temporary repairs gave way and *Teesdale* sank with very little warning, taking with her two of her crew. The rest, with Captain Hill, took to the lifeboats where they spent the next twelve hours in a very rough sea.

This, however, did not end Captain Hill's sea-going career for he was soon given a new command, *Pikepool*. On 14 February 1918 the ship left Rouen for South Wales under convoy. Somehow a submarine penetrated the destroyer screen and *Pikepool* was torpedoed in her number two hold. The stokehold and engine room rapidly filled with water and the order was given to abandon ship. The crew took to the boats but when they saw their ship was not going to sink they returned and, with the assistance of a tug, took her safely into Portland where she arrived the next day. For their services in getting the ship to safety gratuities were awarded by the Merchant Ships Awards Committee, ranging from £75 for the captain to £8 for the firemen.

After the war, when Captain Hill was presented with the Shipping Federation's gold medal by William Ropner in the presence of all the staff, William observed that in his view bravery in the face of the unknown was of a much higher order than bravery on the battlefield amid shot and shell. Even he, William added, conceived it possible that he might show a spark of courage in the thick of severe fighting in the field amid the accompanying roar of guns; but cheerfully to face the ever present dread under which merchant seamen lived during the war, of being blown up by an enemy which might not even be seen, demanded, to his mind, a much higher degree of pluck. After handing over the medal William then commented that he knew how most brave men hated such occasions and that therefore he would not oblige the captain to make a speech. 'Thank you, sir,' said the captain and, as the local paper described it, 'there the pleasant little ceremony ended.'

Another victim during that terrible month of April 1917 was *Daleby*. Under the command of Captain Charles Hord, she left Huelva on 5 April bound for Garston with a cargo of ore when she was torpedoed without warning off the coast of Ireland. Apparently, she went down immediately taking her captain and all but two of the crew with her. One of the survivors, Gunner Wilson, swam about for two hours before he eventually found one of the ship's boats and managed to scramble into it. He then searched amongst the wreckage strewn across the water and found another survivor, Fireman Davies, but no one else. They were both picked up eventually by a steamer which landed them at Avonmouth.

With the introduction of the convoy system shipping casualties fell dramatically – to 226 Allied and neutral ships in July, to 155 in September and to 116 in November. The numbers rose again during some months of 1918, but by October, the month before the Armistice, they were down to under sixty. But although the

U-boat menace was slowly conquered the toll on the Ropner fleet continued. In June 1917 *Westonby* was torpedoed and sunk 195 miles south west of the Fastnet rock; and the same day, the 15th, *Teesdale* was torpedoed off Prawle Point whilst on passage from the Tyne to Gibraltar. In both cases there were no casualties amongst the crews. Government tugs came alongside *Teesdale* and began to tow her bow first towards Salcombe. She became so much down by the head that they had to tow her stern first but could not prevent her from grounding on the Salcombe bar. The tugboats then cast off but the ship's master, Captain J. W. Green, managed to get her off as the tide was rising. The tugs then came alongside again and she was eventually towed over the bar and into shelter. She was repaired at Devonport but, as previously mentioned, sank while on passage to the Tees.

Four days later *Brookby*, under the command of Captain B. Maughan, was attacked by a submarine about a hundred miles off the Scilly Isles while on passage from Sagunto. She was shelled for some considerable time and was eventually hit. *Brookby* fought back but when she began to sink the crew, five of whom had been wounded, took to the lifeboats and were later picked up by a patrol boat and landed at Falmouth. The two apprentices on board, J. F. R. Stanley and S. F. Kingsland, behaved splendidly by assisting the master and gunners during the action, and both were later highly commended for their meritorious conduct. Unfortunately, Stanley was seriously wounded during the battle and was no longer able to go to sea.

After having three ships disabled or sunk in one month it was as well for the firm that its next casualty did not occur until 15 September when *Rollesby* was sent to the bottom by a submarine. Under the command of Captain Donald McKenzie, she had left Lerwick on 15 September in a convoy bound for the White Sea. Within an hour of the escorting destroyers leaving the convoy a submarine attacked it. The leading ship was sunk immediately by a torpedo and then the U-boat turned its attention to *Rollesby*. It began by shelling her and although Captain McKenzie used his smokescreen the submarine managed to get to windward and continued to pour its gunfire into her. *Rollesby*'s gunners returned the fire but the range was about five miles, too far for the ship's gun to be accurate. The captain wirelessed for assistance but could get no reply and when the submarine started firing shrapnel, which did a lot of damage, the decision was taken to abandon ship. Soon after the crew had taken to the boats a destroyer was sighted. Thinking they were safe, the crew returned to their ship and after repairing a damaged steam pipe the engines were restarted. However, the submarine proved to be persistent and while the destroyer was still in the area it fired a torpedo at *Rollesby* which hit her on the starboard quarter. The crew returned to the boats and twenty minutes later the ship sank. Captain McKenzie later reported to the firm that to his knowledge seven steamers had been sunk off Lerwick in three days.

The next casualty was *Teespool* which left the Tyne on 15 October 1917 bound for the Mediterranean with a cargo of coal. When about three miles off Dartmouth she was torpedoed and severely damaged. Part of the crew took to the boats immediately, but four of the crew, including the fourth engineer, lost their lives when one of the boats overturned. The master, Captain J. N. Chard, stayed on board with the remainder of the crew and although the ship was making water rapidly they managed to run her ashore at Dartmouth in a sinking condition. For saving their ship the Merchant Ships Awards Committee awarded Captain Chard £75 and three quarters of a month's pay to the rest of the crew who had remained on board.

Teespool was the last Ropner ship to be lost by direct enemy action in 1917, but on 23 December of that year *Romanby*, in convoy from the U K to the Mediterranean, broke her wheel chains and was hit by another vessel when she sheared off to port. The collision flooded the engine room and after five hours she sank.

The first Ropner ship to encounter the enemy in 1918 had a lucky escape. *Mountby*, under the command of Captain Austin, had lost her convoy when on passage from Milford Haven to Gibraltar in February 1918 when she saw a submarine attack another steamer which was on her starboard quarter and about three miles from her. At about the same time they picked up a broken S O S which they presumed came from the stricken vessel. An S O S was transmitted giving the other steamer's position and the decks were cleared for action. Shortly afterwards a submarine was sighted heading towards *Mountby*, but a smokescreen was laid and evasive action taken, and after half an hour the ship was able to resume her normal course. Half an hour after that, however, a periscope was sighted on the starboard beam and once more a smokescreen was laid and evasive action taken.

Mountby was now in contact with the U S destroyer *Dale* and a description of the first submarine and the other steamer was transmitted. After the destroyer had left the ship's area to search for the submarine and for survivors from the other steamer the submarine shadowing *Mountby* was seen to be approaching them from the starboard bow. Again, a thick smokescreen was laid down and kept going until darkness fell and nothing more was seen of the enemy. *Mountby* eventually arrived at Gibraltar without a scratch on her.

Not so lucky was *Maltby* which was in convoy in the Mediterranean under the command of Captain John Olive when she was torpedoed and sunk on 26 February 1918. The third engineer, A. Davison, and three Arab firemen were killed by the explosion.

The following month *Rockpool*, on passage from New Orleans to Dublin with a cargo of coal, was attacked off the coast of Ireland by a U-boat and sunk by two torpedoes. Only one lifeboat was left for the whole crew and as the master, Captain John White, was rigging the mast the submarine came alongside and took him aboard. The following report by Captain White, written after he had been repatriated, is a vivid account of his experiences as a prisoner-of-war.

He [the U-boat captain] told me people in England were starving and that he was taking me to Germany where I would be able to have plenty to eat. He sent off the lifeboat and the submarine started north keeping about 20 miles off the Irish coast and ten miles off St. Kilda. We passed a submarine going south about 1000 Sunday March 3rd and then passed in sight of the Flannel Islands. They allowed me on deck when I wished to go. After the Flannel Islands we were under water most of the time until we got into the North Sea on account of aeroplanes and patrol boats being sighted. We passed in between Fair Islands and the Orkney's under water. They asked me to tell them where the mines were and I told them I did not know. The Second Lieutenant said it would be better for me to tell them as we might be blown up at any moment, but again I repeated, 'I do not know.' We got safely through the North Sea into the Kattegat, passing the Skaw about eight miles off, at 1000 on the 6th March. At 1800 a submarine came alongside and put some oil aboard, as our submarine was short, but again I was not allowed on deck. At 1900 they completed taking in oil and proceeded.

7th March: Still proceeding through the Kattegat at 0800 I was allowed on deck. At 1100 a periscope appeared right ahead, half a mile off and they thought it was English. They commenced to zig-zag and blow smoke out of the stern. They manned the gun and fired two shots, but missed, and when the periscope was a long way astern the submarine came on top and they found it was German. At 1900 our submarine went under water and remained on the bottom until 2300 off the Kullen lighthouse. They told me that I would not be allowed on deck when she came on the surface until I got permission. All the time she was under water her wireless was working. At noon on 8th March I was given permission to go on deck. We arrived in Kiel at 1700 and took oil on board, sailing at 1800 through the Kiel Canal.

9th March: at 0900 we arrived in Wilhelmshaven with four other submarines, one having another Captain on board. There was a band playing and a number of German officers meeting the submarines. One officer was making a speech but all I could make out was 'Napoleon'. After we went into the dock I was put on the battleship, *Prussian*. I stayed there six days with the Captain who was brought in on the other submarine. The sixth day we were taken separately to the Commander's cabin and he asked me where we made up the convoy when we left the Bristol Channel. I told him that it was out at sea but he wanted to know what part. I repeated my first answer, that it was out at sea. In answer to his further enquiry as to whether they made them up at Milford I replied in the negative and also that I had never been in the place (although at the same time I had). He almost threw me out of his cabin and sent the sentry to escort me back to my room. The next afternoon we were taken ashore to a barracks. At 1700 a sentry gave each of us a basin and he took us to a cook house where we were supplied with paste, the same as is used in England by billstickers. I complained to a clerk in the barracks, asking for something to eat and he said, 'Have you not had anything yet?', and I showed him what the sentry had got for me and he told me that that was all he himself got to eat. I then told him that the submarine commander had told me he was taking me to Germany where there was plenty to eat, but he replied, 'Oh, no, this is all we have got here.'

While on the submarine, I was given a hammock to sleep in, right forward alongside the torpedo tubes and the sweat made the place miserable. I was wet through for seven days. The food on the submarine was potato hash and black bread out of tins. I made chums with the crew and they told me they just went into the submarines because they were compelled to. They asked me if I would employ them after the war and of course I said, 'yes'. They then informed me that when the submarine goes down 50 metres the English depth charge took no effect. They had sunk three steamers before my ship, but they did not know their names. I could not get to know the name of the Commander, this seemed to be secret information.

On the 16th March the Captain of the *Birchleaf* and myself were taken out of the barracks at 1800 and trained to Brandenburg, arriving there at 2300 with half a loaf of black bread for the journey. When we reached the camp we were put into a stable for the night with nothing to lie upon. There were six Russian soldiers in the same place. When daylight broke and we were able to see, we noticed that the Russians were in a pitiable condition with vermin and I felt pleased that I had walked about all night to keep myself warm. We were taken out of this stable at 1000 and taken to an office where we were searched. They also took note of who we were and where we lived. We were then taken to have a bath – a shower bath without soap. The Russians were in the same room but they were given lime to wash with. When Captain Roberts of the *Birchleaf* and myself finished bathing we were allowed out amongst the others. I came across some British bluejackets who told me they were going to be transferred to Holland, so I asked them when they reached Holland to try to get the information through which I had heard on the submarine (U.94) that if they submerged 50 metres, that our depth charge took no effect and that it had three periscopes, a 4.7 gun forward, a 12lb gun aft, four torpedo tubes forward and two tubes aft. Some of the bluejackets were in mufti; one of them left the company but I took little notice of it just at the time, but a little while after a German officer came and took Captain Roberts and myself away, put us in a room by ourselves with a sentry to guard us. We were not allowed to speak to anyone nor anyone to us. They gave us each a bunk with three bottom boards in and two blankets. I had to use my jacket as a pillow. The bed in the bunk was not shavings but small sticks. We were given a Russian soldier to act as orderly who took the bags of sticks out and mashed them down so that I was able to lie on it. The Russian carried our food for us which consisted of potato peelings, boiled in water with the dirt left in, which certainly gave a delightful colour and flavour. An Under Officer applied to the Commanding Officer for the same food for us as the German officers received but this he absolutely refused to do. Fortunately, we had not to eat this stuff as there was an English gunner in the camp who used to pass eatables to us. He assisted us as well as he could. We had a month in this room but were always moving our bunks about to try to find a spot where the cold winds could not penetrate. During that month we had a few hungry days. We were taken out after the month and one morning at 0600 were put in a train for Berlin. We arrived there about 0900 and about 0915 set off again, arriving at another station about 1000. Then we commenced to walk along a country road. After walking about 20 kilometres we were about worn out. The other Captain being an elderly man, it went badly with, causing his feet to be very much blistered. We told the German officer who was escorting us that we could walk no further. He said he could get a cart at a farm if I would pay for it. This I consented to do and he got the cart. We arrived at Pescoe camp at 1800. After being searched we were allowed among other prisoners who were all Romanian officers, no English, and as they got foodstuffs from France they shared them with us. After being there three months parcels began to arrive for Captain Roberts and me from the British Red Cross Sailors Society. I was even more fortunate in receiving a parcel from my owners, Sir R. Ropner & Co. After being there three and a half months the Romanian officers were sent home. Then Captain Roberts and I had a week by ourselves. One Saturday night we heard that British officers were coming in at 2000 from Karlsruhe. Captain Roberts and I were sent away at 1900 to Fort Zorndorf amongst Russian officers where we stayed until about three weeks after the signing of the Armistice. We were then sent to Fort Gauges where we were pleased to have three days with ten British officers and a Colonel. We then got orders for home where I arrived on 14th December 1918.

During the closing months of the war the Ropner fleet continued to be attacked, the last four victims all being torpedoed. *Saxilby* was hit off Malta in May; *Mountby*, which had had such a lucky escape only months previously, was sunk in June; *War Deer*, which, with *War Hind*, had been put under the firm's management that year by the Shipping Controller, was hit off the northeast coast at the end of August; and *Baldersby* was sent to the bottom in September. Both *Saxilby* and *War Deer* were saved and there was no loss of life, and all the hands from *Mountby* were also saved, but *Baldersby* sank with the loss of two of her crew. Her master, Captain Eves, looked as if he was going to have to endure the same fate as Captain White for after the remainder of the crew had taken to the lifeboats the U-boat surfaced and took him aboard. However, after some intense questioning of Captain Eves the U-boat commander said that as he was not returning immediately to Germany he would return the master to his crew.

Baldersby was Ropners' last casualty of the war. By the time the Armistice was signed the fleet of fifty-seven steamers had been reduced to twenty-one.

6
The Great Depression

In 1908, on the occasion of Robert's Golden Wedding, a garden party had been held to celebrate the event. The staffs from both the shipowning and shipbuilding companies had been asked and the office staff at West Hartlepool had presented an illuminated address on which were inscribed the signatures of the staff and their length of service. Mr W. Lancaster had put in twenty-nine years of service; Mr W. C. White, twenty-six years; Mr W. F. Battersby, Mr W. Kirby and Mr C. V. Sutton, seventeen years; Mr T. Barker, fourteen years; Mr J. Nicholson (engineer superintendent), eleven years; Mr J. Thorn (stores superintendent), fourteen years; Mr F. White (assistant engineer superintendent), four years; and Mr P. Dyer, two years.

The celebration of the couple's Diamond Wedding was, however, a much quieter affair – instead of holding another garden party as originally planned they chose instead to give £500 to a local charity. In 1921 Lady Ropner died, a loss from which Robert never really recovered. He was seriously ill in the following year and died in February 1924, aged eighty-five. 'Ruthless, but clever and straight' was how the son of a contemporary summed up his character. Not many of us could earn such a succinctly accurate obituary.

By the time of their father's death John and William, of course, had been running the firm for many years, but even after the war Robert was still to be seen once a week at Mainsforth Terrace and no doubt he had had a hand in deciding in 1915 that the firm should come into line with the new laws which would enable it to trade as a limited liability company. As a result of this decision R. Ropner & Co. became Sir R. Ropner & Co. Ltd, and all the ships that did not belong to the Pool Shipping Company were transferred at the beginning of 1916 to the management of the new company. And for the first time in the firm's history two non-family directors, Mr W. C. White and Mr T. Barker, were appointed directors, while Mr Thwaites, who had been with Robert since the beginning, became Company Secretary. Mr White died in 1921, having served the firm for thirty-nine years. Mr Barker also served the firm for the rest of his life. He had joined in 1895 and in 1905 had moved to the London office for a seven-year stint as a chartering clerk. In 1921, when Mr Thwaites retired, he became Company Secretary of all three Ropner shipping companies, a job he held until he died in 1938.

In 1919 it was decided to bring the running of the ships further into line with modern practice by forming the Ropner Shipping Co. Ltd. This was founded to own all those ships which were still owned under the now outmoded 'sixty-fourths' system. It started with thirteen ships and an issued capital of £1.3 million, with its steamers being managed by Sir R. Ropner & Co.

The world in which Ropners found itself in 1919 was very different to the prewar years. Up to 1914 the UK merchant fleet had expanded rapidly, and, although by as early as 1900 its percentage of the world steamer tonnage started to decline as other countries began building their own, it still owned 44 per cent – or 18.9 million gross tons – of the world's total at the outbreak of hostilities. The UK's nearest rivals at this time were Germany, with 5.1 million gross tons, and the United States and Norway with 2 million. It has been estimated that international trade in 1912 amounted to between 250 and 300 million tons, of which 150 million was either exported from or imported to the UK. British export of coal alone amounted to 77 million tons, and this almost certainly provided employment for as much as 2 million gross tons of UK tramp steamers, as well as a good deal of foreign tonnage.

In contrast to this dominant position in 1914, by the Armistice the UK fleet had been cut nearly in half – to 9 million gross tons – by enemy action, and although some of this had been replaced by new construction the total was still 3 million gross tons less than it had been in 1918. In fact, the UK fleet did not regain its prewar level until 1921 by which time its percentage of world tonnage had dropped to 35 per cent, and it continued to decline so that in 1939 it was 28 per cent.

On a smaller scale West Hartlepool in 1914 had probably been the country's premier tramp shipowning port. No less than forty-four firms had had their head offices registered there and these controlled 232 ships amounting to 700,000 gross registered tons. Many, of course, only owned one or two steamers, but there were quite a few with five or six, and several, like George Pyman, the West Hartlepool Steam Navigation Company and Furness, Withy, were considerably bigger – though Ropners was still by far the largest. Yet by the time the war had finished the number of firms had been reduced to ten, controlling just forty-four steamers. Some, including Thomas Appleby, went into voluntary liquidation, while others gave up, having lost not only their ships but the young family blood needed to run them. Many were deterred from building up a new fleet by the incredibly high cost of construction.

The reason for the exorbitant prices for new construction was the world-wide shortage of shipping in 1919. The lack of capacity to carry global peacetime trade created a vacuum into which speculators willingly plunged, both buying secondhand at highly inflated prices and building new for just about any sum the construction yards quoted. As a consequence, some Tyne owners simply sold what remained of their fleets lock, stock and barrel to Cardiff speculators at handsome profits – and then bought them back a few years later at one fifth the price.

Into this hazardous economic and trading situation Ropners sailed with extreme prudence, for at the helm it had wise pilots well tutored by their father in avoiding the shoals and rocks onto which quick profits lured so many. The firm almost certainly ended the war in as sound a financial position as at the start, but without having made any of the great profits which had come the way of some. The cause for this was threefold: the war insurance on steamers was so high that, as one of the Pool Shipping Company's annual reports pointed out, the whole of a voyage's profits could be swallowed up by them, even after government assistance. Secondly, at the outset of the war the government had requisitioned ships as and when it needed them. Rates of hire for these charters, the so-called 'Blue Book' rates, were fixed in October 1914 and varied according to the type, size and speed of the steamer. Not surprisingly, the rate fixed by the government was a modest one, but in 1915 the 'Blue Book' rate and the free commercial rate were roughly comparable. By 1918, however (by which time 96 per cent of all cargo was being carried at the government rates), the free-market rate had quadrupled, but the government had raised the 'Blue Book' rate by only a fraction of that. This meant that the much higher costs of running the ships – wages had risen by 80 per cent since 1914 and coal prices for bunkering had doubled – had to be absorbed by shipowners.

Thirdly, and from the point of view of new construction, the most important drawback for shipowners like Ropners was that the compensation for war losses of requisitioned ships was based on an estimate of their future earnings at requisitioned rates, not on their replacement cost. Consequently, the sums paid in compensation invariably fell far short of what it would cost to rebuild a similar ship. As a result, Ropners only built two ships during the war, *Swainby* in 1917 and *Sedgepool* the following year. *Swainby* cost £73,428 against the £58,769 a similar ship had cost in 1913. A year later the difference was even more marked, with *Sedgepool* – just 12 per cent larger than *Swainby* – costing a staggering £149,520. However, the cost of these two ships was more than recouped when *Hartlepool*, which had cost about £45,000 in 1909, was sold after she had been requisitioned for use as an oil-carrier for the huge sum of £260,000. This money formed a useful reserve for the company from which the directors were able to increase its capital by issuing bonus shares. When the government put up for sale several standard-specification steamers that had been built during the war (some of which the firm had managed for the duration) neither William nor John considered purchasing them to replace their own war losses. They considered them stop gaps – which subsequently proved to be right – and preferred to trade with the ships they had until the construction market turned in their favour. However, when the German merchant fleet was handed over, two of its steamers, *Hornfels* and *Germanicus*, were managed by the firm for a short time until *Germanicus* was wrecked on Bricquette Island, Gulf of St Lawrence, in November 1919 and *Hornfels* was sold in 1920.

Besides being blessed with cautious directors, Ropners was also lucky in other respects. Unlike many families in which the younger generation had been decimated on the battlefields, both William's sons, Leonard and Guy, came home from the war, as, eventually, did all the office staff. Both Leonard and Guy were demobilized as majors, having fought with the Royal Artillery in France. Leonard commanded a siege battery for two years and took part in the fighting in the Ypres salient, and at Loos, Arras and other places, and for his bravery was awarded the Military Cross. Guy was gassed while fighting and after returning to England became a gunnery instructor at Dover Castle. In September 1914 Mr Percy Dyer and Mr Harry Deane were among the staff who volunteered for the army. Mr Dyer, a future director, was wounded in 1916 and the following year was captured. Another future director, Mr William Wiley, who had joined in 1915, volunteered in 1917 and had just completed his officer training when the war ended.

Guy entered the office in 1919, but when the railway strike took place the same year he left his desk to work with the Northeast Railway Company until the emergency was over. Later, he became a local councillor and by the late 1920s was the director in charge of all the firm's chartering. Leonard also started working for the firm in 1919 but only on a part-time basis as in the spring of that year he took up a scholarship to Clare College, Cambridge, which he had won when at Harrow. He took a degree in Political Economy in only five terms as was allowed at the time under special regulations for ex-officers. Both brothers were made directors on 1 January 1922.

Leonard was, perhaps, the most extrovert of the four brothers, and newspaper clippings show him to have been not only a noted public figure but a keen sportsman. He rowed, he skiied, he shot, and by 1923 he had won no less than six cups racing at Brooklands, but his big passion was undoubtedly politics. After starting in local politics in 1923 he stood as parliamentary candidate for Sedgefield where, after three recounts, he won the seat by six votes, one of the only two seats in the country during that election to be won by a Conservative from Labour. The following year he increased his majority to 1600 and at the end of 1924 was appointed Parliamentary Private Secretary to the Secretary of State for War. 'I am assured in Conservative inner circles that Major Leo Ropner, MP, JP, is considered as one of the rising hopes of his party,' wrote a gossip columnist in 1925. 'He is a giant – a huge and splendidly built man with almost auburn hair and that schoolgirl complexion which is the sign of health.' Once he became an MP he was, of necessity, more involved in politics than in the day-to-day running of the firm. He was, however, from his earliest days in Parliament, a staunch supporter of the shipping industry and although he could no longer work at West Hartlepool he continued to attend the London office every morning in addition to his parliamentary duties.

The West Hartlepool office during and immediately after the war is within the living memory of several retired members of the firm. Mr Charles Ringwood gives an especially vivid picture of it.

I started work with Ropners on 2 January 1916. I got the job because Mr Barker knew the headmaster of my school and he asked him if he knew anyone who would make a suitable office boy. Funnily enough I'd always wanted an office job and had even learnt shorthand before leaving school. I couldn't type – I'd never even seen a typewriter – but I could do 100 words-per-minute in shorthand. My salary was £10 a year paid monthly. My main duty apart from running up and down to the post office about a mile away was to make sure in the evening that the gas lights were lit and then go outside and make sure no lights were visible which might attract German bombers. We were very understaffed when I started because of the war and we brought in a Miss Austin to help out, the first girl we ever employed. Battersby was another clerk in the office. He used to do Mr William's letters. When he joined up in 1917 I took over his job. I hadn't been in the office more than 18 months and I would type the letters with two fingers. But I learnt something new every day – that's one of the beauties of shipping. I learnt something new every day of the 60 years I was in it.

Sir Robert would come in about once a week to attend to his correspondence. He had a man called Lancaster who looked after him. When he came into the office I'd hear the bell ring. 'Get me a glass of vater,' he'd say, a phrase that was known throughout the office even after Sir Robert died!

His son, John, was very well dressed, very gentlemanly in everything he did though he was a bit autocratic. Later on, when he became Sir John after his father died, he became less active in the firm and he'd only come in in the mornings. His brother, William, was my boss. He was very humane, very compassionate, a thorough gentleman, very highly principled. He was ramrod straight and always very just in his dealings with others. One day a Norwegian pilot came into the office. At the time I was in charge of the petty cash and Mr William told me to give the pilot £2 and put it down as extra pilotage. The pilot had had to land in the Tyne as it had been too rough to land in Norway and he had had to come all the way back to England. But he had to get back and Mr William thought £2 would be enough. I saw the pilot look down at his shoes and knew he wasn't happy about it. Then later when they'd talked in Mr William's office they both came out and Mr William told me to give the pilot £4, and the pilot said happily, 'that's better than noding'. Mr William was always very fair.

When I became a clerk I would write up voyages. If a ship with, say, coal sailed from Hartlepool to Genoa and was then chartered from Istanbul to America, that was a cargo out to Genoa, then in ballast to Istanbul, then a cargo across to the United States. When you got in all the accounts after four or five months from the Captain you wrote them up in a ledger. You wrote it in longhand and you had to balance the accounts of that voyage to the last penny. Everything was set out. Sundry expenses first, then you'd get expenses at Hartlepool for loading the coke. You'd put it all down and the commissions. Then you'd put down the charter commissions, then the expenses to Genoa – you might stop at Gibraltar, for instance – then you'd put the Genoa expenses and the Istanbul ones and so on until the ship got home. We did an enormous amount of business carrying grain from Montreal. The ships would go out in ballast – though sometimes they'd take coke or anthracite – and then they'd bring back grain. When you had one voyage like this it didn't take long to balance the books because there was only one cargo.

In fact, the young Ringwood – and Ropners – was lucky to have voyage accounts to make up in this period, for after the boom year of 1919 freight rates began to slump alarmingly. During 1920 the monthly time-charter rate dropped from 46s per deadweight ton to 14s, a sure sign that the good times were over. However, worse was to come for the following year the existing rates were halved. The annual report of the Pool Shipping Company of 1921 referred to 5 million tons of shipping lying idle and stated that 'we regret to say that during the past few months the freight market has gone entirely to pieces and remunerative employment is practically unobtainable.' Nevertheless, a dividend of 20 per cent was paid, although the following year this dropped back to 15 per cent, but the profits came not from its twelve steamers but the sale of government securities sold for a substantial gain. By August 1922, however, the Ropner Shipping Company was warning shareholders 'that there may be a period during which the Company will be unable to pay a dividend'. In recommending a 5 per cent dividend for the year the directors stated this was only made possible 'because of a substantial gain upon investments realized during the year.' In other words, the wise policy of the directors in building up the reserves of both companies was now more or less keeping those companies in existence and profitable.

The following year the dividend dropped to 2½ per cent in the case of the Ropner Shipping Company and 10 per cent for the Pool Shipping Company. In 1924 they paid 2½ per cent and 10 per cent respectively, but in 1925 the Ropner Shipping Company did not pay a dividend at all and was obliged, because the value of tonnage had fallen to such a low level, to reduce its capital by a third, by bringing down the value of its shares to 13s 4d. The Pool Shipping Company, better placed to weather the appalling state of international trade because it had had much longer to build up adequate reserves, again paid out a 10 per cent dividend, despite the annual report's remark that 'the homeward markets are worse than at any period within our memory'.

In 1926 the Ropner Shipping Company paid out a 2½ per cent dividend although the directors noted that the shipping trade remained depressed and that this depression had been increased by strikes, not only in Britain but in other parts of the world, notably Australia and South Africa. They added, however, that the amount of tonnage building was comparatively small and that 'we can only look patiently forward for the long-deferred improvement'. The Pool Shipping Company again paid out 10 per cent.

To some extent the improvement the directors were looking for occurred during 1926, but this was mainly due to the National Strike when coal had to be imported into the country. The Pool Shipping Company declared a 15 per cent dividend and the Ropner Shipping Company 6 per cent, a figure the latter company held to in 1928 although the Pool Shipping Company dropped back its dividend to 12½ per cent, dropping again to 10 per cent in 1939, while the Ropner Shipping Company still held to 6 per cent. The

Pool Shipping Company's dividend dropped to 7 per cent in 1930 and then no dividend was paid at all until 1936 when a recovery in trade, more or less sustained until the outbreak of war in 1939, enabled a small dividend of 2½ per cent to be declared. The Ropner Shipping Company paid a 2 per cent dividend in 1931, the last declared until 1936.

The annual reports of both companies are bleak documents, but they accurately reflect the depth of depression during those terrible times. For fourteen years or more the prospects for shipping – that most sensitive barometer of global prosperity – seemed grim indeed. The hard times being passed through by the industry were emphasized over and over again by William during this era. For instance, at the beginning of 1927 he pointed out that, although some tramp owners had done well as a result of the coal strike, the extra cost of bunkers and the delays caused by the General Strike often swallowed up the entire profit of a voyage. He doubted if there was a 3 per cent return on the capital invested by tramp owners, and that 'had it not been for the strike an optimistic view of the coming year would have been justified.'

Troubles abroad as well as at home created further difficulties and a year later we find William saying that

> the Australian market has been sadly disappointing to shipowners, and will certainly not recover its popularity until the fear of labour troubles out there be allayed, and until it becomes possible to make voyage calculations with a reasonable probability of anticipations being realized. No owner today can calculate within £600 or £700 what his expenses at the loading port or ports will be. In any event he must reconcile himself to the fact that the charges at the Australian ports will be at least three times as heavy as, for instance, at Montreal.

Against such a background it would be reasonable to suppose that even the most optimistic person would reckon the industry had little future and would act accordingly. With the Ropners, however, the very opposite reaction occurred, and an observer can only marvel at the strength of conviction, surely inherited from Robert, in the two brothers, and later in William's sons, which gave them the foresight to start and maintain a building programme the size of which had not been seen in the firm before or since. It made sound economic sense, of course, but only if the principals had, as

John and William must have had, a total commitment to the industry with an unwavering belief that eventually it would prosper once more.

The purchasing of new steamers started in a modest way when *Roxby(2)* was bought in 1923 from a bankrupt company while still on the stocks at the Ropner yard at Stockton. She was not the normal type of ship operated by Ropners, being 7680 tons dw, but she was bought at a very reasonable price and served the firm well until torpedoed in 1942.

This purchase looked as if it might be the last for some time, for in their 1923 annual report the directors remarked that 'the moment in our opinion has not yet arrived for adding materially to the fleet', and the next acquisition was merely the management of a steamer called *Onaway*, which was disposed of in 1924. However, by the end of 1923 tonnage prices had slumped so much that the directors, acting on their father's policy of building when prices were low whatever the state of the freight market, ordered for delivery in 1924 five new steamers. These were *Salmonpool*, built by Irvine's Shipbuilding and Dry Docks Co. Ltd, *Rudby*, built by Wm Gray & Co. Ltd, and *Bridgepool*, *Reedpool* and *Drakepool*, all constructed at the Ropner yard. Apart from *Willowpool*, delivered in May 1925, these steamers were the last to be built for the firm by the Ropner Shipbuilding Company as it was sold in 1925, having built for its sister company no less than seventy-one ships. A few years later it was demolished as part of the industry's national plan to reduce capacity.

Apart from *Willowpool*, only *Ainderby* was constructed in 1925 for the firm, and was followed in 1926 by two more, *Firby* and *Otterpool*. In this year and the following one five of the older pre-1900 steamers were sold off, this generating extra capital to pay for the six vessels delivered in 1927. These were *Warlaby*, *Troutpool*, *Romanby(3)*, *Rockpool(2)*, *Ullapool* and *Ashby(2)*. Eleven more followed in 1928 and three in 1929. The programme was then really completed though a further nine ships were built for the firm during the 1930s and five second-hand ones added to the fleet to replace the ten sold or scrapped between 1928 and 1935.

This huge reconstruction of the Ropner fleet generated the somewhat cynical joke that Ropners built their steamers by the mile, chopped off sections, gave them names, and called them ships! But, as someone commented in the company magazine two decades later,

They were efficiently run and efficiently managed, and continued at sea during the depression long after more fanciful vessels were tied up in creeks and backwaters as non-competitive.

In fact this joke had little validity, for the steamers produced from 1928 onwards were far better designed, with finer lines, longer hulls and a deadweight tonnage of 8750, and from 1929 they had superheated boilers, more powerful engines, and were an additional 16 feet in length, giving them a deadweight tonnage of 9235. The first of this new type was *Heronspool*, and so economical did it prove to be that most managed to keep trading during even the worst of the depression, and in 1933 it was decided to improve the economical running of the older steamers as well. Nothing could be done about the hulls, but in May 1933 Wm Gray modified the existing triple expansion engine belonging to *Swainby* to use superheated steam and this experiment proved to be such a success that later the same year it was announced that the engines of fourteen of the firm's older vessels would be similarly converted. Less successful – a disaster in fact – was the Brand's Patent Pulverised Fuel Company's efforts to introduce this type of propulsion to the Ropner fleet. They converted *Swiftpool* to burn pulverized fuel, but after two trips she was converted back to coal burning at Brand's expense.

Where the firm might have seemed conservative in updating its fleet was the insistence on retaining coal as the fuel for its ships. There were, however, sound reasons for doing this. 'We have confined ourselves entirely to steamships,' William commented when announcing in July 1927 that the firm had ordered eight steamers during the previous twelve months at a cost in excess of £600,000, 'and not diesel-engined or oil-burning vessels, in order that the coal industry might benefit', and the following year he added a further reason. 'The initial cost of a motor-ship,' he said, 'is much greater than that of a steamship of similar size, and it has yet to be shown by actual experience that the expenses of the engine department of putting a motor-vessel through her periodical surveys when she attains to a ripe old age (say, 16 to 20 years) will in any way compare with that of a steam vessel.' It is interesting to note that in the period he made these remarks the price of coal had dropped by 17 per cent while oil had dropped only 5 per cent. Within a few years, however, the economic argument for retaining traditionally powered, triple expansion engined steamers was not so clear-cut and, in the years 1935 and 1936, two new turbine-driven ships, *Clearpool* and *Hawnby*, and two motor ships, *Moorby* and *Wearpool*, were delivered.

By modernizing the fleet John and William kept the firm on the solid foundations their father had so carefully laid down prior to the First World War, and as a result their ships were able to take advantage of whatever small upturns in trade occurred. After the Wall Street crash of 1929 this became harder and harder to achieve and between July 1932 and July 1933, for instance, no less than thirteen Ropner ships were laid up for some period, *Holtby*, built in 1909, for 273 days. Even the more modern steamers did not escape entirely and seven of them were tied up for short periods. Voyage records show that even when a ship continued trading the profits were minimal and there was often a loss as the following examples illustrate:

Saxilby: Swansea/Montreal, 6/6d, followed by T/C Jacksonville/Continent, 60c, thence Tyne. Total round of 98 days, of which the ship lay idle at Swansea four days awaiting commencement of laydays, and was for three days lying unfixed in the St Lawrence. Profit per day – £1-1s-0d.

Ainderby: From Tyne unfixed to Newport, Mon., thence coals to Alex. 6/-, followed by Marioupol/Manchester and Barry 12/9d. 104 days. Ends meet.

Rockpool: Barry/Savona 6/10½d. Huelva/Baltimore 11/1½d. 28 days T/C del. Baltimore, redel. Norfolk 85c. Baltimore/Antwerp 7½c per 100lbs. thence Tyne. 124 days. Loss £230.

Stonepool: Tyne/Genoa 6/4½d. River Plate/Las Palmas and London on the berth, average 14/6½d. 110 days. Loss £303.

These figures tell their own story of the struggle to survive and they do not, of course, include the firm's running costs like repairs, annual charges for surveys, depreciation, interest on capital, and so on.

As a result of these appalling trading conditions the firm turned to time-chartering in the Canadian coal trade. After lengthy negotiations with the Dominion Coal Company two twenty-year-old vessels, *Kamouraska*, renamed *Coalby*, and *Wabana*, renamed *Canby*, were purchased in 1931 by the Ropner Shipping Company and time-chartered to the Dominion Coal Company. The trade was a hard one which demanded especially well-built steamers capable of standing up to rough usage in loading and discharging and both ships had been in it for a long period before being purchased by the firm. They were supplemented the following year by a new ship, *Domby*, which was specially constructed, with special steel hatches, and she proved to be a particularly stout boat in heavy weather. The contract for her time charter coincided with the one to build her, a practice common nowadays but almost certainly an innovation for the firm in 1931.

By 1930 the induction of the third generation of the Ropner family into the firm was complete. William's third son, John Raymond, Jock to everyone, joined the Hartlepool office on 21 September 1925, after studying at Cambridge and winning a golf blue (he was a scratch player); and his fourth son, Robert Desmond, joined on 20 September 1930, also from Cambridge for which he played squash racquets. Jock became a director on 1 June 1928 and Robert on 1 January 1935, by which time, of course, the fourth generation was well on its way. In 1921 Guy had married Margarita Gray and the firm's chairman up till 1984, William Guy David, known as David, was born in 1924. Jock was the next to marry, in 1928. His first son, William, chose not to enter the firm, but his second son, Jeremy, born in 1932, is now the senior director in charge of the Shipping Division of Ropner PLC. Both Leonard and Robert married in 1932. Leonard's son, Sir John Ropner Bt, is now the senior director responsible for the firm's fast-growing Property Division. Robert's eldest son, Bruce, is the senior director overseeing the firm's engineering interests, while his second son, Garry, is joint managing director of Ropner Insurance Services.

7
Tragedy and Triumph

By 1932 the firm had rebuilt its fleet to fifty, the largest number it was ever to own after the First World War, thirty vessels being owned by the Pool Shipping Company and twenty by the Ropner Shipping Company. It was a modern fleet – the ships averaged about ten years in age – and it was again one of the largest in the country.

A proportion of the new vessels ordered replaced those sold or scrapped as being uneconomic, but a few had to be constructed to replace losses that occurred during the inter-war years. William always maintained, half jokingly, that bad luck struck three times. With the loss of three steamers in the early 1920s this belief was upheld, but when two more were lost in the early 1930s under far more tragic circumstances, no one must have been more relieved than the senior director that the theory was proved wrong – although, as will be seen, a third tragedy was only averted by magnificent seamanship.

The three casualties in the early 1920s occurred when *Wandby* stranded at Kennebunk, Maine, in the spring of 1921; *Troutpool* went ashore at Newfoundland in September 1923 during fog, broke her back and had to be abandoned; and in December the same year *Somersby*, off course as it had been impossible to take any bearings for two days, hit the Baldoyo Bank near Corunna and became a total loss. Fortunately, in none of these incidents was there any loss of life and considering how great were the hazards of the sea in those days the firm's record during the inter-war period was extraordinarily good and between 1923 and 1933 no other ships were lost. Perhaps the nearest escape occurred in 1927 when *Otterpool*, loaded with coal, caught fire in the Indian Ocean. An explosion blew the hatches off the number four hold and then the fire quickly spread to the number five hold. Fighting it became nearly impossible as all the canvas hoses became chafed and useless in the gale-force conditions in which the crew found themselves, and soon only one leather hose remained. Nevertheless, the flames were brought under some sort of control, but the fire continued to burn for days after the ship had docked at Adelaide.

Another dramatic incident involved *Deerpool* in the Bay of Biscay in April 1932 when the master, Captain F. C. Berner, managed to rescue four Breton seamen in mountainous seas after they had abandoned their fishing boat. In recognition of the captain's skill in rescuing the Frenchmen the French Government subsequently presented him with a bronze plaque mounted on a mahogany stand.

Between 1923 and 1933 several ships were grounded, one lost its rudder during a gale, and there was the tragic case of a steward being lost overboard, but with this one exception, no other loss of life occurred at sea during this period. However, in November 1933 *Saxilby* (Captain B. J. Samuel) was on passage from Wabana to Port Talbot with a cargo of ore when she was caught in a severe storm 400 miles off the west coast of Ireland. At 0850 on 15 November Valentia radio station picked up the following message from the steamer. 'In position lat. 51.50N, long. 19.15W.: require immediate assistance.' Earlier an American steamer had picked up a message saying that the crew were trying to launch the lifeboats and she, with others including the liner *Berengaria*, converged on *Saxilby*'s last known position. An extensive search was made in appalling weather conditions but there was no trace of either the ship or her crew of twenty-eight.

The following winter brought equally atrocious weather in the North Atlantic in which, as in the previous year, several ships were lost. The worst storm of all occurred in October 1934 and caught in it were not one but two Ropner steamers, *Millpool* and *Ainderby*. On 2 October at 1958 GMT the Belle Isle wireless station received the following message from *Millpool* (Captain Newton) which was on passage from Danzig to Montreal with a cargo of grain: 'Lat. 53.50N., long. 37.10W, after hatch stove in, main topmast gone, three men injured, drifting helplessly before gale, using temporary aerial.' Several ships also picked up this message, including the Cunard White Star liner *Ascania*, which proceeded immediately in hurricane-force winds and 50-foot waves towards the distressed steamer's last position. During that terrible night several further messages were received from *Millpool* confirming her position and adding that the main mast had smashed through the deck and that she was sinking. One of the last messages – 'working on an emergency wireless set' – indicated that the engine room was flooded and the transmissions became fainter and fainter, and by 0200 they had ceased altogether. An intensive search of the area was made but nothing was ever found. An inquiry the following year completely exonerated the owners of any responsibility for the steamer's loss.

It is not possible to re-create the conditions under which the crew of *Millpool* struggled to survive, but luckily *Ainderby* (Captain E. Bestell), caught in the same maelstrom and in communication with the distressed ship, managed to ride out the appalling conditions – and her master's report on the voyage is in the firm's archives.

We left Swansea on 21 September 1934 bound for Montreal with a cargo of 8000 tons of anthracite. The voyage opened with calm seas and fair weather, but as soon as we reached the Fastnet strong SW winds were experienced, with heavy and continuous rain and the sea began to rise, until when barely out of sight of Ireland I had to heave to and reduce speed for the safety of the ship. The same weather continued with slight intervals until the 28th when, in lat. 53.26N., 26W, the sea rose with such fury the vessel became practically unmanageable.

Then occurred the first, and to my mind the greatest of our misfortunes. On that day at 1120 one of our young apprentices was washed overboard from the foredeck. The officer on watch immediately grasped the situation and released the lifebuoy which was on the port side of the bridge and at the same time several members of the crew let go other lifebuoys at different parts of the ship with the hope that one would float within reach of the boy. I at once gave instructions to the Chief Officer to have the lifeboats ready and turned the vessel round. At the time mountainous seas were running and breaking over the ship, and I very much doubt that even had we seen the boy, it would have been possible to launch a boat. However, everything was ready and if he had been sighted a desperate attempt would have been made to rescue him, in spite of the sea and weather. Unfortunately, when the vessel was turned round we steamed between the first buoy and the apprentice's cap without seeing any sign of him. I could only come to the conclusion that he had gone down. Nevertheless, I did not let this idea stop me, but searched for fully three hours, though the vessel was being continously swept by heavy seas . . .

From then to the 1 October the ship was hove to practically the whole time, being unable to make headway against the terrific seas which were battering her. We made our best run from noon on 1 October to noon on the second when we were in lat.52.14N., 41.20W. Then a dark cloud spread over the sky and the sea rose with renewed force. We had to heave to again and only with great difficulty were we able to keep head on to the sea.

At 1415 on that day, when I had just left the bridge to change my wet clothes, a tremendous sea struck the vessel, carrying away both bridges, the engineroom telegraph, stoving in no:1 hatch and knocking the man at the wheel unconscious. I immediately rushed on deck and climbed up on the remains of the bridge. The first thing I noticed was the Second Officer emerging from the wreckage, his face streaming with blood where he had been struck by wood and glass from the broken bridge.

The other officers had followed me on deck and we at once realised the gravity of our position. By this time the helmsman had regained consciousness and was once more at the wheel though badly shaken. I saw there was only one thing to do however dangerous it might be. Water was rushing into no:1 hold and the ship was settling by the head, bringing the rudder and propeller out of the water. I must turn round and risk being overwhelmed in the trough of the sea, otherwise the vessel must surely be filled with water and sink in a very short time.

I first sent a radio message to all ships in our vicinity to stand by and was answered by the Cunard liner, *Antonia*, and the Hain steamer, *Trematon*, which were however at a considerable distance, but advised me that they were proceeding as quickly as possible to my given position. I also received the following message from another of our Company's ships, the *Millpool*, which read: 'Helpless myself driving before hurricane since 1pm Noon 53.38N . . .' This unfinished message suggested that the *Millpool*'s aerial had carried away before the operator had time to complete it.

I then instructed the Third Officer to have all hands not otherwise engaged mustered in the engineroom and had it battened down so that no one need be unnecessarily exposed to the risk of being washed overboard or injured by the sea while turning. I also instructed him to tell the Chief

Engineer to give me all the steam possible and to start pumping the water out of no:1 hold.

While this work was being carried out an SOS message was received from *Millpool*. Knowing that his crew had enough to worry about, Captain Bestell instructed the wireless operator not to tell anyone about the SOS and to tell *Millpool* that he was unable to help as they were themselves in a desperate plight.

Now came the critical moment when all our lives depended on how the ship would respond to my endeavours. I gave the order hard to port on the helm and the vessel started swinging sluggishly. When she came into the trough of the sea she appeared to lay for what seemed an eternity. She shipped another sea into no:1 hatch which was wide open and I began to fear we would not get round before being overwhelmed. However, the vessel proved her excellent qualities of strength and seaworthiness and gradually came round until we had the sea right astern . . .

We all heaved a sigh of relief when the vessel came round and I particularly, though I knew our troubles were by no means ended. I then advised those ships standing by for me that I had successfully turned and to proceed on their respective voyages.

No:1 hatch now had to be secured and only those who have experienced similar conditions at sea can realise the danger of this task. Green seas were continually sweeping over, and to make matters worse, on going forward with the crew, the Chief Officer reported that the iron bulkhead in the well deck had also been stove in and water was rushing through the 'tween decks to the stokehold.

To enable me to cover no:1 hatch I ordered the hatch boards to be removed from no:2 which being on the bridge deck, and consequently higher, was not so much exposed. Fortunately, there was very little alteration needed to fit these boards to no:1. The men commenced sawing the boards on deck, but after several seas were shipped over them I ordered the board to be taken into the engineroom and sawn on the cylinder tops. This done they commenced the dangerous and difficult task of fitting them to the open hatch and covering it up. My state of mind can be imagined at this time. One sea like the one that disabled us would have swept the whole crew into the sea but the situation was desperate and I had no alternative.

As it happened we shipped a big sea over the poop which carried everything before it, flattening all the ventilators, flooding the store room containing our provisions, shifted both lifeboats on to the engineroom skylights and stove in the cabin door. By this time the force of the water had been somewhat expended and when it engulfed the men at work on no:1 hatch they were all able to hang on except the Chief Officer who was swept off his feet and badly bruised against the iron bulkhead. The men picked him up unconscious with blood running from his mouth and brought him along to his cabin, which through the bursting of the cabin door was flooded with water almost up to the bunk. I asked the steward to attend to him as I and the other officers were fully occupied. No doubt his absence was keenly felt but the others had to carry on as best they could.

By dusk number one hatch had been covered and a temporary covering put on number two hatch, but by then the water was halfway up the number one hatch coamings and the ship was badly down by the head with her propeller barely touching the water. Nothing could be done to repair the iron bulkhead in the forward well deck and water continued to flow through the 'tween decks into the stokehold. At 0400 the chief engineer reported that the lower fires on the boilers were in danger of being put out as the water was washing through the ashpits, and that soon he would have to withdraw the firemen. Without power to keep the ship's stern to the waves, the captain knew they were doomed, so he withdrew the pumps keeping the water out of number one hold and transferred them to the stokehold bilges. This had the desired effect and by morning the captain was able to return the pumps to number one hold, but his troubles were still far from over.

During the morning I noticed the rudder was jamming and sent the Third Officer to investigate and he reported that the quadrant was bent to the deck. You can imagine the force required to have bent such a massive piece of iron. The deck plates had to be cut away to allow the quadrant to move to and fro. This work was entrusted to the Bos'n and Carpenter who were made fast by ropes to prevent them being swept away by the sea.

The rest of the crew under the Third Officer were sent to shore up the after welldeck bulkhead to fortify it against the heavy pounding of the sea, in order to prevent a similar occurrence to what had happened to the bulkhead in the forward well. This work had to be carried out under the most trying conditions. The men worked battened down in no:4 hold, by the faint light of hurricane lamps and the knowledge they had that at any moment a sea might stove in the bulkhead, made the coolness with which they carried out the task all the more to be admired, for if such had happened they would have been trapped like rats in the rush of water which would have flooded the hold.

Wireless messages concerning the steamer's plight now began to be received in *Ainderby*'s wireless office, which was itself awash almost up to the operating table. One to the captain was from his wife and simply said, 'Courage beloved.' That evening he signalled the firm that he would have to abandon his voyage and asked permission to return. This was immediately granted along with a suggestion that he should receive towing assistance. By now, however, Captain Bestell had gained such confidence in his ship that he replied that he would try and reach port under his own steam. Before long, though, more danger presented itself.

That night we were still running before the sea which was continually pounding over us, when suddenly I heard a loud report, like a shot from a gun. I sent the Second and Third Officers to investigate, but owing to the amount of water on deck they could not locate the cause in the darkness. At daybreak the next morning, 4 October, we found that the fiddley casing and the bridge deck plating had cracked right across the ship. This must have been caused through the vibration caused by the engine racing, which was so great that the iron plates could not stand the strain. I immediately decided to bring the sea a little on the port quarter thereby easing the strain. This I found worked successfully although a tremendous volume of water came aboard and flooded the cabin amidships. However this was better than allowing the vessel to break her back altogether.

I could not ascertain how far the crack went on account of the bunker coal, but considerable water was pouring through into the 'tween decks and then down to the stokehold. This added greatly to my worries which were not lessened when the Chief Engineer came and told me that the thrust block was loose and several of the bolts were broken, which I understood was a very dangerous thing as the whole thrust of the vessel was taken up at this point.

In the evening the Steward sent for me to come to see the Chief Officer. Leaving the deck in charge of my Third Officer for a few minutes I went down below for the first time for about 53 hours. In the accommodation the scene that met me was one of indescribable confusion. Water was rushing through the officers' cabins carrying all sorts of floating debris. I waded into the Chief Officer's cabin and found him lying with his head propped up on pillows, as white as a ghost, still with blood coming from his mouth, which led me to believe he was bleeding internally. I applied ice to his chest and gave the Steward instructions to do his best as I could not stop longer, but had to supervise the work on deck. Not long after the Steward sent word that the Chief Officer had stopped bleeding and I gave orders to bale out his room as much as possible and put dry bedclothes on his bunk, though where he was going to get them I could not think . . .

The crew's accommodation which was in the fore part of the ship was completely wrecked and inundated with water, and the only place they could go was in the engineroom top. Here, on the gratings they had to snatch a few hours' sleep in turns, when they could be spared from their duties. Since the ship was disabled they had had no regular meals but sustained themselves with an occasional piece of bread or biscuit, taken in their hands. Though they were wet through and the iron gratings could not have made a very comfortable bed, not a word of complaint escaped them. They were a fine body of men, a typical sample of British merchant seamen.

The next morning, 5 October, the weather began to improve and though soundings in number one hold showed there was still some fifteen feet of water in it the worst was now behind the battered vessel and her exhausted crew. Later in the day a sextant reading showed the ship had been blown over a hundred miles south of her supposed course and a new one was set for the nearest port, Queenstown. By midnight, however, the water in the number one hold had dropped sufficiently for the propeller and rudder to grip the sea properly and the master decided to make straight for Swansea. At 0300 on 8 October they were abeam of the Fastnet and made the Mumbles at 1515 where the ship was met by several tugs and a pilot.

'In conclusion,' wrote Captain Bestell,

I must put it on record that all our efforts must have ended in failure had we not had such a splendid ship under us which had been fully equipped in every respect with all the necessary spares and stores. In answer to the critics in the House of Commons who have ignorantly termed this class of ship 'the slums of the sea', I can only say that I hope for nothing better than to spend the rest of my sea career in one of these 'slums', as I shall always have a warm spot in my heart for the *Ainderby* after her gallant and successful battle against the worst the Atlantic has to offer.

The triumph of saving *Ainderby* from the Atlantic is by no means unique in the annals of the Merchant Navy – nor, probably, in the history of Ropners – but her story is worth repeating at some length here not only because the master's graphic description of what happened has survived but as an example of just what seamen of that generation sometimes had to endure. For Ropner seamen, however, the next great challenge came not from the sea but from the Nazi U-boats of the Second World War. They rose to it with some surprising results.

8
Ropner's Navy

By the mid-1930s William's four sons were all well established in their careers. Leonard, after being defeated in the 1929 election at Sedgefield, had won the Barkston Ash seat in 1931. During his first spell in Parliament he had not spoken a great deal but throughout the 1930s he was frequently on his feet in the House, more often than not to support the needs of the shipping industry whose views he represented very ably throughout this period. Guy and then later Robert both became interested in the Chamber of Shipping, while Jock chose to concentrate on running the business from the office in Mainsforth Terrace. All four sons were each given eight ships to manage and William kept eight himself – though by the time his brother died in 1936 he himself was only attending the office in the mornings. When Mr Barker died in 1938 Mr P. W. Dyer, Mr W. Wiley and Mr C. Ringwood were all appointed managers, and Mr W. Kirby, who had joined the staff in 1891, became Company Secretary.

It has been estimated that by July 1932 no less than 13.5 million gross tons, or 20 per cent of the world's shipping, was laid up, and most maritime countries took some action to aid this section of their economy. In Britain, help came late in the day – not until 1935 in the form of a subsidy – but in the years leading up to this government action both William and Leonard were tireless writers to *The Times* about the perilous position in which the British shipping industry found itself. In the Chamber of Shipping Guy campaigned hard for a subsidy to be introduced, while Leonard made several speeches in the House of Commons on the same subject.

Eventually, the 1935 British Shipping (Assistance) Act was passed through Parliament. Under its terms a fund of £10 million was made available for 'scrap and build' loans, and provision was made for up to £2 million to be paid out in the form of a subsidy for freight rates. If the rates fell below the level of 1929 then the difference was made up from the subsidy. This assistance was given on the understanding that the industry formed a suitable organization for administering the fund. This resulted in the Tramp-Shipping Administrative Committee being formed along with various subcommittees for negotiating minimum freight rates. Leonard became a member of the Administrative Committee and also of the Far East/Pacific Trade Subcommittee, Guy was appointed to the St Lawrence Trade Subcommittee, and Jock to the Australian Trade Subcommittee.

The subsidy was in operation during 1935 and 1936. It was also renewed for 1937 by the government but was not used as the level of freight rates rose above the 1929 minimum. However, the recovery in trade was not sustained and in January 1939 Guy Ropner was writing in the *Newcastle Journal* that

> 1938 has been a very disappointing year for shipowners, but comfort can be taken from the fact that never has the industry, the tramp section of it at any rate, been so united in its aims and never has the Government shown greater willingness to appreciate the gravity of the situation. During the whole of 1938 freight levels have been extremely low, and simultaneously costs have continued to rise, so that it has been impossible, except in the controlled trades, to run vessels so as to make depreciation, and certainly not depreciation and a profit.

Both the Pool Shipping Company and the Ropner Shipping Company benefited by the subsidy in 1935 and 1936, but the 'scrap and build' subsidy was not used by the firm. Two ships were scrapped in 1935 and one in 1936 but as their combined tonnage did not exceed the new tonnage built during those two years neither company was eligible for financial support.

At the outbreak of war in September 1939 the Pool Shipping Company owned twenty-six ships and the Ropner Shipping Company nineteen, totalling 403,611 tons dw. The years of mounting political crisis during the late 1930s had ensured that the British Merchant Navy was much better equipped to fight than it had been in 1914. Many ships had already been stiffened aft to receive the defensive armament with which they were hurriedly fitted once war was declared. Despite the acute shortage of escort vessels the convoy system was also immediately reintroduced.

Plans had also been made beforehand for the dispersal of shipping offices inland in the case of war. A large empty house in Sedgefield, called The Whins, was earmarked for Ropners, and on 4 September 1939 the move from West Hartlepool was started. Within a few days it was 'business as usual' – though the fact that the only available telephone for some weeks was a few doors down in the local pub must have temporarily inhibited even the most efficient members of the staff!

However, Mainsforth Terrace was not closed completely as both the stores and marine department remained, and a future director of the London shipbroking office, Chris Jackson, vividly remembers joining the firm while the 'phoney' war was still in progress.

I went down on my bicycle and remember being very impressed by the office building with its brass plates on the door and the insignia of the company flag on one of the windows. Inside was a hall with a very large staircase. On the staircase landing was a very large window with the Company's arms on it. One went into the general office through swing doors and then one came to a counter. In the office there were high sloping desks with stools to sit on and flaps that lifted up. Across the top was a brass rail where one used to put the ledgers. In addition to the stores and marine departments there was what was called the sail loft on the top floor. This was the place where the tarpaulins were made for the ships' hatch covers. It was manned by a Captain Thomson, who wore a bowler hat fixed firmly on his head, a walrus moustache, and canvas dungarees he'd made himself. To help him he had a man called Carter and a boy called Harold. They used to take in these huge bolts of canvas by a hoist at the back of the office which were then made into tarpaulins and so on. They would sit there with the canvas on their knees and their palms in their hands, and they greased the twine with wax and they would sew all the tarpaulins for the ships and all the canvas for the hatches. Then they were all parcelled up and taken to the station on a cart which Harold used to push all by himself. The sail loft was at the top of the office and had skylights, and when we heard that a ship was coming in we would climb up to watch. I remember once seeing *Clearpool* coming into William Gray's yard for repairs after being bombed.

A last glimpse of a world which was about to disappear for ever.

Initially, Ropner ships were only directed by the Ministry of Shipping with the firm undertaking to do their utmost to supply, at any time of emergency, vessels as and when and where required, whatever the inconvenience. However, within months Ropner ships were once more being requisitioned, resulting in the firm losing all financial interest in their voyages. To Jock this inevitably meant a loss of efficiency in running the fleet and he protested to the Minister concerned but to no avail.

The first Ropner loss came within a week of war being declared when the 3000-ton *Firby* left the Tyne in ballast for Hudson Bay to load a cargo of grain. As the convoy system was then not in full operation she went north about to avoid known submarine areas of operation. On the fourth day out – 11 September – soon after she had reached the Atlantic, a U-boat surfaced half a mile astern of her and opened fire. *Firby* had not yet been armed and all she could do was to start zigzagging. But the range was short and the Nazi's gunfire was accurate, and after several men had been wounded the master, Captain Prince, stopped his engines and he and the crew took to the lifeboats. The U-boat closed in and Captain Prince was ordered aboard. Some papers were taken from him, but he was given some bread and some bandages for his wounded men, and then he was returned to the lifeboats. After the U-boat had dived *Firby* blew up and after fifteen hours in the boats the crew were rescued by HMS *Fearless* and landed at Thurso.

The next U-boat attack on a Ropner ship found the latter better prepared than *Firby* had been. *Heronspool* left Swansea on 6 October 1939 loaded with coal for the St Lawrence. After joining her convoy, which included another Ropner ship, *Stonepool*, she steamed westwards. By 12 October, however, she had lost the convoy and was on her own when she saw, at a distance of about six miles, a U-boat shelling what turned out to be a French oil tanker. Curiously, it would have been against international law for the master, Captain Batson, to try and intervene. Instead, he obeyed his standing orders and turned away. The 4-inch gun on the poop was manned and the lookouts doubled. As darkness fell the French tanker burned brightly. It was a dark night with no moon and for a while the master thought they might have escaped. But then from astern a light flashed, ordering them to stop. Instead, Captain Batson kept his ship moving at top speed and sent out an SOS. For half an hour nothing happened and then, at 2030, the U-boat opened fire. Ranging on the gunflash the ship's gun crew fired back. They got in two shots before the U-boat, surprised, perhaps, at being fired at, dived. Nearly two hours went by before the U-boat surfaced again and fired on the ship from its port quarter. The gunners on *Heronspool* only had the chance to fire one shot before the submarine submerged once more. It reappeared at 2300, but again the gunners could only loose off one round before it vanished. For an hour the crew waited, and worked to get every last ounce of speed out of their ship in the hope that they might keep the submerged U-boat astern to prevent it from launching its torpedoes. But at around midnight there was a huge explosion just ten yards or so from the side of the ship. The crew never knew what caused it, but guessed the U-boat's first torpedo had exploded prematurely or had hit an object just before penetrating the ship. The U-boat now surfaced once more and zigzagged from quarter to quarter, firing as it went. None of the shells came near *Heronspool*, whose gun returned the fire. For half an hour this continued before the U-boat broke off the engagement, dived, drew abreast of the steamer and launched a second torpedo. This struck the forepart of the ship and the force of the explosion ripped the hull apart and broke the ship's back. Luckily, none of the crew was in the fore part of the ship and no one was injured. After a battle which had lasted four and a half hours Captain Batson was forced to give up. He stopped his engines and he and his crew took to their lifeboats. Just before dawn *Heronspool* sank and soon afterwards the American liner, *President Harding*, picked them up and landed them in New York. On 15 December 1939 it was announced from Buckingham Palace that for their bravery during this prolonged action Captain Batson had been awarded the OBE and the gunner, Able Seaman George Pearson, the BEM.

At about the same time that Captain Batson and his men were being picked up by *President Harding*, the first officer of *Stonepool*, then just beyond the horizon to the south, sighted a U-boat on the surface just forward of the ship's port beam and about three miles distant. *Stonepool* had broken away from her convoy to make her own way south to the Cape Verde Islands with her cargo of coal and machinery, so she was quite unprotected except for her own armament of one 4-inch gun mounted on the poop and a light anti-aircraft gun. The master, Captain White, immediately gave orders for the ship to swing away from the U-boat, and as *Stonepool* started to alter course the submarine fired its first shot. Within moments the ship's gun began to fire back, but shortly afterwards *Stonepool* was hit forward just above the waterline and began to make water. Minutes later another shell smashed the port lifeboat, but the submarine then dived. In the minds of the crew there was little doubt as to what would happen next.

The lookouts saw the track of the torpedo a long way off and Captain Batson managed to swing his ship out of its path. The U-boat now surfaced again and the two vessels recommenced firing at each other. Before long, splinters from a near miss destroyed the ship's second lifeboat and there were other close misses. The U-boat now began to move from quarter to quarter, swinging almost broadside on before firing, thereby giving the ship's gunners a much larger target to aim at. Quite why it did this the crew could not guess but it proved to be the enemy's undoing for *Stonepool*'s fifteenth shell appeared to hit the submarine. However, this did not prevent it from submerging and this it immediately did. The time was now 0635 and the first part of the action had lasted fifteen minutes with the submarine firing eighteen shells. Another fifteen minutes went by and then the U-boat resurfaced in more or less the same position. It was well astern, but the master managed to see through his binoculars that the enemy's gun had been hit and was now half lying over the side.

The U-boat now began to make wide zigzags and lifted itself higher and higher out of the water by blowing its tanks. 'She came up so high she looked almost like a destroyer, she had so much freeboard,' said one of the crew later. It looked almost out of control and did not attempt to pursue the ship. After a while its hull dropped below the horizon but at 1015 it reappeared on the port quarter about five miles away. For about an hour it steamed along with *Stonepool* but when the ship altered course away from it it again disappeared from view.

With his vessel noticeably down by the head, Captain White now turned his attention to the shell-hole forward. Soundings were taken of number one hold and it was found to be flooded to the depth of 10 feet. The coal was dug away from the hole and a temporary patch placed over it, and then the pumps were switched on to clear the water. On deck other members of the crew began to patch the one remaining lifeboat so that if the ship sank under them they would have some chance of surviving. At 1200 the ship was still making water and Captain White decided to abandon his voyage and return to the Bristol Channel. Shortly afterwards a destroyer hove in sight, having picked up *Stonepool*'s SOS. She steamed past them at top speed and disappeared in the direction of the U-boat's last known position. A few hours later she returned and signalled: 'Good work.' 'From that,' Captain White commented afterwards, 'and the presence of about six miserable-looking men huddled together on her deck, I formed the conclusion that the sub had been destroyed.' In fact, the U-boat had been scuttled by its crew as soon as the destroyer had appeared and later Captain White received the following signal from C.-in-C. Plymouth: 'Congratulations on your escape you have set a fine example have contributed directly to the destruction of the submarine do not break wireless silence unless you require assistance.'

Escorted by the destroyer, *Stonepool* made for safety. It is reasonable to assume that Captain White and his crew now felt that the worst was behind them. However, the threat of both the enemy and adverse weather conditions was still there and soon after the destroyer had taken up station on *Stonepool*'s starboard bow one of the ship's lookouts spotted a U-boat surfacing on the port quarter in just the position where the ship's hull hid the submarine from the destroyer. The signal 'U-boat port quarter' was flashed urgently to the destroyer which immediately swung away to engage it. The U-boat crashdived after several salvoes from the destroyer but was then destroyed by depth charges.

With the sinking of this second U-boat *Stonepool* had now helped even the score between Britain's enemy and Ropners, and had avenged the sinking of *Firby* and *Heronspool*. But *Stonepool*'s troubles were not over for on Sunday, 15 October, while still leaking badly, she encountered strong winds and a rough sea. The destroyer had been obliged to leave her the previous day and as she pounded through the heavy weather the remaining lifeboat was partly carried away. Water now began to fall on the cargo in number one hold and the pumps had to be kept constantly at work. They managed to stem the inflow and at 0715 the next morning they dropped anchor in Barry Roads. In December Captain White was awarded the OBE for 'his resolute and skilful action', and the gunner, Able Seaman Frederick Hayter, was awarded the BEM.

On the very same day that *Stonepool* fought her successful duel with the U-boat, another Ropner steamer, *Rockpool*, in a convoy of ten ships out of Newfoundland and loaded with ore, was battling against a full Atlantic gale. At 0500, well before dawn, her port lifeboat was partly carried away and her master, Captain Harland, signalled the commodore of the convoy for permission to heave to. In the darkness and the severe weather conditions they could not make contact with the commodore but Captain Harland decided to heave to anyway. The lifeboat was retrieved, but at dawn *Rockpool* found herself alone. She failed to find the convoy again and by 19 October had entered the Western Approaches, an area extensively patrolled by U-boats. On returning from his lunch below to the bridge Captain Harland at once saw a U-boat to starboard and as he gave urgent orders for the ship to swing away the submarine opened fire.

Captain Harland later reported to his owners:

I ordered the helm hard a port, called all hands to their stations and sent out a radio. He fired four or five rounds very quickly but did not get a hit. We opened fire and at the third shot he submerged. After about three or four minutes he commenced to rise. As soon as his periscope came above the surface we opened fire. He fired several rounds of shrapnel, the shells bursting just clear of the bows. We got close to him. Through the binoculars you could see the spray from our shells going over his conning tower. He again submerged for a few minutes. The battle went on like this until 1345. He was working out a very good bracket and at any moment I expected to be hit. When we dropped our shells close to him he dived. At 1345 I ordered smoke floats to be thrown over the side. At 1350 the smoke screen was effective and we got away without damage to the ship or crew. I must in concluding say the morale of the crew was astonishing, there was no panic, every man carried out instantly the orders that were given. At 1600 I put the firemen on double watches and kept them doubled until we passed Lundy Island. This was the only way they could keep a full head of steam. Stores lists etc. will be forwarded tomorrow.

To this dispassionate account of a battle fought over more than ten miles Captain Harland added a brief postscript. 'Since writing the above letter, I have been informed by the Admiralty that we so damaged the submarine that he could not submerge. A destroyer coming in answer to my radio captured the survivors and sank the submarine. I did not see the destroyer.' In December 1939 Captain Harland was awarded the OBE. The citation for Captain Harland's decoration read:

A U-boat suddenly appeared on the beam at about one and a half miles distance, and immediately fired a shot which fell about 100 yards short. The second shot was close on the quarter. The Master at once altered helm to bring the U-boat astern and his gun into action. He fired thirteen rounds, which fell so close that the enemy was drenched with spray. The U-boat fired some twenty rounds, and *Rockpool* was straddled, but not hit. After a stern chase of an hour and a quarter she shook off the enemy by zigzagging behind a screen of smoke floats. The crew showed great coolness under fire, and all who could helped in the action. The Master handled his ship in a seamanlike manner and deserves great praise for his coolness and judgment, and for the readiness and efficiency of his ship's company. The U-boat, which he was the first to sight, was in due course destroyed by the Royal Navy.

In a similar citation the *Rockpool*'s gunner, ex-Colour Sergeant Thomas Watkins, Royal Marines, was awarded the BEM.

During these early months of the war there was some debate about how best to operate the merchant fleet and the Ministry responsible for it. In the House of Commons on 15 November 1939 Mr Shinwell raised the question of appointments to the Ministry of Shipping and another Labour MP stated that unless the Minister of Shipping took complete control of the merchant fleet large profits were bound to accrue to the owners. At once Leonard was on his feet. His speech was short but to the point and was well summarized by *The Times*.

Colonel Ropner said that in spite of the increased freight rates there was no profit and in many cases substantial and heavy losses. Long detention of ships had been experienced in every case. The convoy system, efficient as it was, led to delays and voyages were taking twice as long as in normal times. While these conditions existed neutral tramp ships were being chartered by the Government at fantastically high rates of freights. The British Mercantile Marine was in a position entirely inadequate to the needs of the nation.

He paid a tribute to help given to merchant shipping by the Royal Navy. Two of his company's ships had been sunk by submarine; two others were attacked but gave such a good account of themselves that they disabled two German submarines, both of which were finally sunk by destroyers within a few hours of breaking off with the Mercantile Marine. At the Admiralty 'Ropner's Navy' was almost as well known as that of his Majesty. (Laughter and cheers.)

A legend had been born.

9
Taking Up the Fight

In the five and a half years that followed the two epic battles between Ropner's Navy and the Nazi submarine fleet Ropner seamen were awarded no less than thirteen OBEs, along with three BEMs and two Lloyds' medals for bravery, but the loss of ships and lives was severe. At the start of the Second World War Ropners owned forty-five vessels; by the end of it only eleven remained afloat. The firm also managed a number of Dutch, Yugoslav, French and Norwegian ships, as well as over forty vessels for the Ministry of War Transport, and the casualty rate amongst these was also high. But the most tragic statistic was the loss of life, with over 600 seamen serving with Ropners being killed.

Ironically, however, the next casualty was only indirectly the victim of war. *Deerpool*, bound for Hull, arrived off the entrance to the Humber after dark on 12 November 1939. There were warnings of a submarine in the vicinity. Although in wartime many navigation lights were not displayed and many ship's masters would have considered it unsafe to enter an estuary like the Humber at night-time, the Ropner master decided that doing so was the lesser of two evils. Unfortunately, this did not prove to be the case as she stranded near Spurn Point and became a total loss. From the insurance point of view the vital question was whether she was lost as a result of a war risk while seeking to escape from a submarine or whether she was lost by a straightforward marine peril in stranding. In the end the marine underwriters paid the claim.

Eleven days after the loss of *Deerpool*, *Willowpool* left Bona with a cargo of iron ore for Middlesbrough. On 10 December, when near her destination, she struck a mine and sank within a few minutes. All the crew were rescued though three of them were injured.

Though U-boats were the greatest threat to merchant ships, many were attacked from the air. *Otterpool* had two narrow escapes early in 1940. On 29 January, while approximately four and a half miles west of Bell Rock, an enemy aircraft appeared from the east and opened fire with its machine guns, riddling the ship with bullet holes. The 12-pounder high-angle anti-aircraft gun was immediately manned but two of its crew were soon wounded. An SOS was sent out and rifle fire opened on the aircraft from the bridge. In all it made seven strafing runs before being driven off by British fighters. Altogether, ten bombs were dropped on *Otterpool* but all missed, although two were so close they flooded the after-well-deck poop and the gun platform. The following month, on convoy to Norway, *Otterpool* was again attacked from the air, this time by three enemy aircraft. Four bombing runs were made at the ship from different directions but heavy defensive fire was put up and all the bombs fell wide. Sadly, *Otterpool*'s luck ran out in June 1940 when she was torpedoed eighty miles southeast of the Scillies whilst on passage from Bona with a cargo of iron ore. Sixteen members of the crew were picked up, but the remainder, including the master, Captain Prince, and all his officers except the chief officer, were lost.

Another occupational hazard during wartime for merchant ships were German raiders. *Haxby* left Glasgow on 6 April 1940 for Corpus Christi to load a cargo of scrap iron. On 24 April she was approached by a ship flying the Greek flag which suddenly opened fire on her. The German raider, *Orion*, a 7000-ton liner of the Hamburg Line, hit *Haxby* with her second salvo, smashing her gun and killing the gunner. For half an hour the raider pumped shells into the helpless steamer. Sixteen of the crew were killed and the remainder had to swim for it. They were picked up by the raider, which then finished off *Haxby* with a torpedo. The master, Captain Arundel, and his crew were kept imprisoned on the raider for three months before being transferred to a Norwegian ship which had been captured by the raider. Under the supervision of a German crew, the Norwegian ship was making for Bordeaux when it was intercepted by a British submarine and Captain Arundel and his men were rescued and landed at Gibraltar.

Mines were also a great danger to shipping and during 1940 several Ropner ships were lost after hitting them: Captain Harland, who had fought and damaged a U-boat whilst master of *Rockpool*, had *Hawnby* sunk under him on 20 April, luckily without loss of life; *Troutpool* went down in Belfast Lough on 20 July with the loss of eleven of the crew; and *Pikepool* sank in the Bristol Channel on 22 November along with seventeen of her crew, and the master, Captain Atkinson, and some members of the crew were drifting on a raft for six days before being rescued.

Two months previously *Pikepool* had been involved in the dramatic rescue of eighty-three seamen when their ships had been sunk under them in mid-Atlantic by U-boats. When *Pikepool* reached Newfoundland with these survivors Captain Atkinson wrote a report to his owners which is worth repeating here in full as an illustration of the horrors that had to be faced by all merchant seamen in wartime.

Shortly after midnight, ship's time, 20/21 September, when six days out from S, a radio message was received from *Elmbank* stating she had been torpedoed, position some few miles to the westward of *Pikepool*'s position. Shortly after, a similar message was got from the *Blairangus*, in a position somewhat nearer to us.

At 0200, 21 September an eastward convoy was met head on, although *Pikepool* was following prescribed route. After extricating ourselves from this we proceeded westward again, extra lookouts being posted and gun's crew closed up. At daybreak a vessel was observed ahead and on approach it was apparent she was one of the ships as her stern was blown away and she was awash aft. Two lifeboats were next met which contained her survivors. They were got on board and their boats hoisted on deck. The vessel was the *Blairangus* and had been one of the convoy already referred to. The survivors numbered 28, including the Master, the six other members of her crew having been either killed by the explosion or drowned after being trapped in their quarters as the ship was struck right aft by way of the men's accommodation. The Master assured me their fate was certain so I carried on. Seven of those picked up were injured, two critically, two seriously, and many were suffering from shock, especially those from aft. All were at once given every possible attention and made comfortable. Shortly after, a second steamer was sighted ahead, evidently in a sinking condition. As before, all due action was taken for *Pikepool*'s

Sir Robert Ropner – the founder – c. 1890

William Ropner, grandfather of the four present family directors, 1893

Opposite top left: Robert Ropner, 1865. *Opposite top right:* Mary Anne Ropner, 1870.
Opposite below: Sir Robert and Lady Ropner on the occasion of their Diamond Wedding, 26 July 1918

William Ropner a photograph taken approximately 50 years later than that on previous page, after a long and successful career in the shipping industry

S.S. *Barlby,* 3,680 tons dwt. Built by Ropner & Sons, Stockton in 1895. She was sold to Greeks in 1926 and continued to trade for various owners until over sixty years old

S.S. *Trunkby,* 4,100 tons dwt. Built by Ropner & Sons, Stockton in 1896. Sunk by gunfire from the German submarine 'U34' 50 miles south by east from Port Mahon, Minorca, on 25 May 1916

S.S. *Teesdale,* 3,680 tons dwt. Built by Ropner & Sons, Stockton for J A Wood & Co, West Hartlepool in 1904. She was purchased by Ropners in 1908. On 15 June 1917 she was torpedoed in the English Channel and beached off Salcombe. Soon after recommissioning, she foundered on 2 August that year, three miles north of Saltburn Pier in Yorkshire

S.S. *Thornaby,* 2,600 tons dwt. Built by Ropner & Sons, Stockton, and delivered in 1889. On 28 February 1916 she struck a mine laid by the German Submarine 'U3' and sank soon after

S.S. *Firby,* 8,670 tons dwt. Built in 1926 by William Gray of West Hartlepool, yard no. 979. She was torpedoed and sunk by the German submarine 'U48' on 11 September 1939 south-west of the Faroe Islands

S.S. *Deerpool,* 9,130 tons dwt. Built by William Gray in 1930. Stranded near Spurn Point on 12 November 1939, she became a total loss

Above: S.S. *Heronspool,* 10,490 tons dwt. Built in the USA during 1942 as the *Ocean Valour.* She was purchased by the Company in 1949 and renamed *Heronspool.* Sold in 1955, she was eventually broken up in 1967

Below: M.V. *Daleby,* 7,846 tons dwt. Built in 1950 by James Laing of Sunderland. The first new ship ordered for the Gulf Cargo Line, she carried twelve passengers. In 1961 she was sold to Yugoslavia and traded until 1972

M.V. *Thornaby,* 18,270 tons dwt. Built by James Laing of Sunderland in 1955. *Thornaby* was the first oil tanker to be owned by the Company. The vessel was sold to Greeks in 1966

M.V. *Stonepool,* 45,027 tons dwt. Built in 1966 by Connell of Glasgow and sold in April 1982

Sir Leonard Ropner

Sir Guy Ropner

Mr Jock Ropner

Sir Robert Ropner

ROPNER & Co
THE POOL SHIPPING Co
LIMITED
THE ROPNER SHIPPING Co
REGISTERED OFFICE
LIMITED

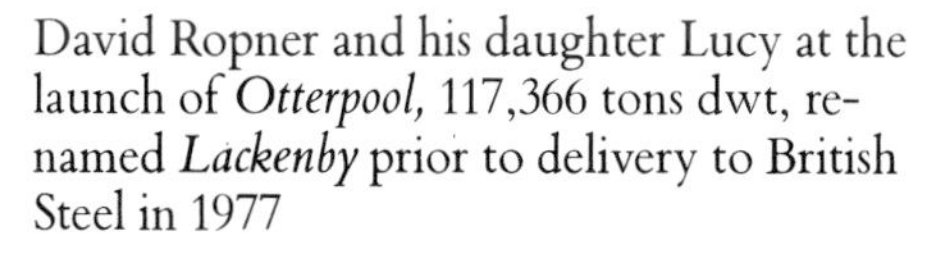

David Ropner and his daughter Lucy at the launch of *Otterpool,* 117,366 tons dwt, renamed *Lackenby* prior to delivery to British Steel in 1977

Bruce Ropner

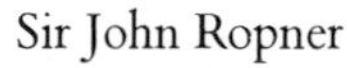

Sir John Ropner

Opposite above: William Wiley, Percy Dyer and Charles Ringwood, company managers. This photograph was taken in front of the new office, 140 Coniscliffe Road, Darlington in 1946. All three later became directors

Opposite below: George Filby and Bill Gidley soon after rejoining the company after the War. They were demobbed in 1945

An aerial view of the Airtech and Hozelock factories taken in 1982. The land in the foreground also belongs to the Company and forms part of the old Thame airfield

Opposite above:
Jeremy Ropner and his daughter Sophia on the occasion of the launch of M.V. *Salmonpool* in 1981

Opposite below:
140 Coniscliffe Road, Darlington, Co Durham. Purchased in 1945 immediately after the Second World War, this building has now been head office for forty years

M.V. *Salmonpool,* 43, 108 tons dwt. Built by Eleusis in Greece in 1982

Falklands Communication Centre, manufactured by Airtech in 1982

own safety on approach, and simultaneously with seeing three lifeboats under sail steering for us, a large ocean-going class U-boat was sighted some two miles distant in surface trim. Our gun's crew were still closed up, of course, at the ready, and the submarine was brought to bear astern in our gun sights whilst the occupants of the three boats were got on board as quickly as possible.

Owing to the nearness of the submarine, *Elmbank*'s boats were abandoned and with all possible speed we proceeded executing 'scatter' zig-zags. When last seen the enemy was gradually submerging some three miles distant. These three lifeboats contained 55 survivors of *Elmbank* and the dead body of her Master who had had both legs shot away. He was reverently buried at sunset that evening. No others were missing or injured seriously, but many were suffering from shock. All were made comfortable. The 55 consisted of 17 whites and 38 of their native crew of Lascars. Their vessel had been hit by two torpedoes and 31 shells, and it was while her Master had been lowering one end of a boat crammed with men that he had been hit by a shell and fell into the boat himself, dying very soon after. Two submarines had attacked her. This vessel had also formed part of the same convoy none of which had been detailed off to ascertain extent of damage to either vessel or plight of their crews.

The German invasion of Norway led to the loss of *Swainby*, which was torpedoed on 16 April whilst on passage to Narvik, and of *Romanby* and *Salmonpool*, which were both captured. *Romanby* was subsequently sunk by the Germans and the master, Captain Nicholson, and his crew were taken prisoner, but they were eventually released and told to walk to the Swedish border. However, the chief officer, Mr Henry, volunteered to take a Norwegian ship through the German blockade and, along with thirteen of *Romanby*'s crew, he evaded capture and eventually arrived in England. Three other members of the crew escaped aboard another Norwegian ship, but when, in June 1942, Captain Nicholson and twelve of his crew tried to bring a Norwegian ship to England from Sweden the vessel was sunk and Captain Nicholson and his men made prisoners-of-war. The master of *Salmonpool*, Captain Yare, and his crew were also interned in Germany. Their ship was renamed *Putsig* and remained in commission throughout the war. When peace came she was retaken at Bremerhaven, renamed *Empire Salmonpool*, and put under the management of the firm until she was sold in 1947.

The next two Ropner ships to be sunk were both being managed by the firm for the Ministry of Shipping. *Empire Merlin* was the last ship on the port quarter of a convoy when at 0153 on 25 August she was hit aft by a torpedo. She broke in two at once and sank, taking with her nearly all her crew, including Captain Simpson who had fought a U-boat so valiantly in 1917 when master of *Wandby*. The only survivor from *Empire Merlin* was in the water nearly three hours before being picked up. After *Hawnby* had been sunk under him Captain Harland was given command of *Empire Bison*. On 8 September his ship survived a bombing attack– 'the warmest half hour of my life' was how the captain described it – but on 1 November the ship was torpedoed in the North Atlantic. Tragically, only three of the crew and one passenger survived, having spent eight and a half days on a liferaft before being picked up.

During the last months of 1940 the U-boat campaign against Allied shipping reached its height and on 19 October Ropners lost two more ships, the brand new motor ship, *Wandby*, on her maiden voyage from British Columbia to the UK, and *Sedgepool*, on passage between Montreal and Manchester. Both ships were torpedoed, *Sedgepool* being one of seventeen ships to be lost from the same convoy.

The first loss in 1941 was *Rushpool*. Two weeks out from Halifax, two torpedoes were fired at her. The first hit her between the cross-bunker and the number two hold and the second blew off her stern. Despite the extent of the damage she stayed afloat for one and a half hours, enabling all the crew to be rescued.

The next to go was the valiant *Rockpool* which had helped destroy a U-boat during the first months of the war. She went aground on Little Cumbrae Island, Firth of Clyde, on 1 February and was declared a constructive total loss. She was later salvaged by the Ministry of War Transport, renamed *Empire Trent* and put under Ropner management until she was sold in 1946.

Twelve days later *Warlaby* was sunk by the German cruiser, *Admiral Hipper*, off the Azores, and twelve days after that, on 24 February, *Mansepool* was hit by a torpedo on the port side by number two hold. The engines were stopped and the crew abandoned ship. Two men were lost and several more injured.

March proved to be an equally disastrous month for the firm. On

7 March *Boulderpool* was torpedoed by an E-boat off Haisboro' Buoy and the following day *Hindpool* was torpedoed north of the Cape Verde Island whilst on passage from Pepel to the Tyne with a cargo of ore. The crew of *Boulderpool* were all rescued, but the master of *Hindpool*, Captain Tinnock, two navigation officers, three engineer officers, one radio officer and twenty-one men all lost their lives. Five days later the Luftwaffe raided Merseyside. Parachute mines were dropped and one landed right on *Ullapool* which had just arrived from Halifax with a full cargo of grain. She sank immediately and her master, Captain Thwaites, the second mate, the chief and fourth engineer officers, the first and second radio officers and nine seamen were either killed or drowned, and four other seamen were injured.

Correspondence shows that Ropner captains now began to voice their opinions about the heavy losses being incurred by the merchant service. On the whole liaison between the two navies during the war was excellent, but on 29 March no less than five ships belonging to one convoy were sunk in the hour and a half between the ocean escorts leaving and the home escorts arriving. The convoy's rear commodore, Captain Churchill of *Bridgepool*, subsequently wrote to the firm asking if something could be done to avoid this gap in time recurring and his complaint was forwarded to Guy Ropner who by then had been seconded to the Ministry of Shipping as its assistant director.

However, during the next Ropner clash with the U-boats the latter did not even bother to wait until the escorts had left. On 3 April 1941 three submarines attacked a convoy in the North Atlantic which included three Ropner ships, *Thirlby*, *Alderpool* and *Daleby*. The results of this combined assault were devastating. Eight or nine vessels were sunk, including *Alderpool*, with *Thirlby* having an escape which was as astonishing as the resourcefulness and bravery of her master, Captain Birch, and his crew. Captain Birch's brief chronological report vividly recreates what happened.

0945: Convoy attacked. British *Reliance* torpedoed. Various left turns.
1100: *Alderpool* torpedoed.
1115: After zig-zag, rapidly, course near *Alderpool* – boats seen in water. Stopped to take survivors.
1130: Survivors almost all on board. Submarine in view on port bow.

Engines working ahead and astern to bring stern on to the enemy.
1135: Survivors all on board. Managed to bring *Alderpool* between this ship and submarine. Full speed.
1140: About ½ mile from *Alderpool* when that vessel struck by second torpedo and then this vessel missed by one across bows and another under stern. Submarine following. Changed course to keep submarine astern when seen.
1245: Submarine about 500 yards on port quarter and diving, but managed to dodge him.
1340: Submarine again on port quarter but again avoided him as submarine dived. Radioed 'ssss de GNRV THIRLBY 58.19N. 28.12W. CHASED BY SUBMARINE.'
1420: Struck by torpedo on starboard side, seen to turn off and go ahead of ship. Submarine for a moment on port side. Obviously there are two submarines in the attack. *Thirlby* now doing over 12 knots.
1455: Submarine sighted astern distance 1000 yards. Fired one round which just went over the top. Submarine crash dived.
1515: Submarine sighted for last time.
1630: Daylight gun manned all through and now crew anxious for further action. Proceeded to steer west and then pulled south.
1800: South westerly course. Complete crew of *Alderpool* rescued and no casualties.

A week later, nearing the end of her voyage, *Thirlby* had an even narrower escape from going to the bottom, but once again the resourcefulness of her master and crew saved her. At 0845 on 10 April the ship was attacked by a plane which was neither seen nor heard until its machine guns and cannon began to riddle the bridge. A stick of bombs was dropped but missed. The bomber circled quickly and attacked again from the stern, with the crew returning its fire with their Hotchkiss anti-aircraft gun. A second stick of bombs was released and one bomb hit the forward well deck, blowing down the foremast and wrecking the bridge. Once more the plane flew round and in its third attack another bomb wrecked the fo'c'sle, killing two of the crew. Captain Birch now ordered his crew to abandon ship in the hope that the bomber, believing the ship to be foundering, would go away. The ruse proved successful and after circling once more the bomber flew off. After twenty minutes or so the crew returned to *Thirlby* and found a fire raging forward and the number one hold flooded. The deck was badly holed and there was a 15-foot rent down the ship's side. Nevertheless, Captain Birch decided to save his vessel if he could and a hose was put on the fire and the hole in the ship's side temporarily repaired.

An hour later the bomber returned and the crew once more took to the boats. However, the plane must have thought the ship doomed for it did not attack again and soon flew off. At 1045 the crew began to return to the ship although a fresh breeze and rough sea had blown one boat four miles downwind. By 1400 *Thirlby* had ceased to settle and as there was no assistance in sight it was decided to proceed. The boats were hoisted and by 1445 *Thirlby* was under way once more making a speed of 5 knots. Despite bad weather and shipping water through the rent in the side, the ship made Loch Ewe safely the next afternoon where temporary repairs were made to enable her to move round to the Clyde.

All through 1941 the destruction continued. On 13 May *Somersby* was torpedoed and sunk in the North Atlantic. All her crew were saved, but when *Ainderby*, which had survived that terrible storm of October 1934, was torpedoed the following month whilst on passage from Brazil twelve of the crew were lost. The same month, June, *Clearpool* lost two of her crew when she was attacked from the air. The vessel was raked with machine-gun fire and then two bombs were dropped, one of which set fire to the bunkers on numbers two, three and four shelter decks. The pipes on the boiler top burst, filling the deck, engine room and stokehold with steam and smoke, and the ship began to fill and heel. A destroyer came alongside and the crew was taken off, but the master, Captain Spouse, his chief and second officers, and the chief and fourth engineers remained aboard in the hope that the ship could be salvaged. The fire was put out and *Clearpool* ceased to settle, and the next morning a tug arrived which towed her to the River Tees. In May the following year the same ship had another narrow escape from being sunk. During the evening of 13 May the convoy in which *Clearpool* was sailing was attacked by a submarine pack. A torpedo was fired at the ship and appeared to the master, Captain Thompson, and to the chief and third officers to be heading straight at the port side by number one hold. However, as it neared the ship the torpedo swerved round her bow and was last seen abeam to starboard. The degaussing equipment was switched on at the time and it is possible that this could have deflected the torpedo. With two lucky escapes *Clearpool* deserved to survive the war, but unfortunately she was wrecked on the Skitter Sands in the River Humber in the middle of 1944.

Another sinking in June 1941 occurred when the only French ship being managed by Ropners, *Criton*, was attacked off the west coast of Africa by a Vichy French warship, and this loss was followed by that of *Swiftpool*, torpedoed in August with heavy loss of life (there were only two survivors), and *Stonepool*, torpedoed on 11 September, also with heavy loss of life.

The sinking of *Stonepool* was witnessed by the master of *Gullpool*, Captain Copping, who was in the same convoy. On his arrival at the Port of London he wrote to the firm:

You remark in your letter that you believe we had a worrying time on our passage from Canada. Well, I don't think the word worrying quite describes our journey. We had the usual experience of fog and ice which is common on that track at this time of the year. This was closely followed by gales in which we suffered slight minor damage, and for the remainder of the passage – this is from Greenland to the UK – we suffered repeated submarine attacks. Our escort worked magnificently but they were totally inadequate for the protection of such a large convoy of 66 vessels, against the large scale and determined attacks to which we were subjected. The main attack began at 2145 on 9 September, and was continuous until 0245 on 11 September. One had a feeling of being like lambs led to the slaughter and just wondering who was going to be the next one to go. My Chief Officer and his gun crew remained at their stations during the whole of this period, snatching a few minutes' sleep as best they could during the lulls in the attack.

Fortunately, I had a good position in the centre of the convoy, immediately behind the Commodore, with the *Yearby* [another Ropner ship] next astern of me. The *Stonepool* was leader of a column on the starboard wing of the convoy and I saw her torpedoed. As far as I know she was carrying grain and had autos in the 'tween decks and on deck, and I have been greatly puzzled as to what caused the violent explosion on board, as flames shot about 150 feet in the air. The whole midship section of the vessel, bridge etc, appeared to us to collapse and she then heeled over on her side. Owing to the darkness and the distance away it was impossible to trace further movements of the vessel but it has greatly shocked me to hear that up to the present only six survivors were rescued. Some vessels remained afloat for about an hour whilst others went down in just so many seconds.

When a ship went down quickly there was little chance of saving those working below. The engineer officers, greasers and firemen were especially vulnerable, as the sinking of *Ashby*, torpedoed on 30 November 1941, shows. Separated from her convoy on account of bad weather *Ashby* was forty miles to the west of the Isle of Flores when she was hit by a torpedo in the vicinity of number five hold. The chief officer only just had time to cut the lifeboat adrift when the ship went under, only two or three minutes after the explosion. Thirty-three survivors were picked up, but among those missing were four firemen, two greasers and all the engineers, as well as the master, Captain Frank, the second officer and five seamen.

Nineteen forty-two proved to be as disastrous for the firm as the previous year had been. In January *Thirlby*, which had twice managed to avoid being sunk in 1941, was torpedoed in the North Atlantic with the loss of three of her crew. Then on 1 March there occurred for the firm the worst single tragedy of the war when *Carperby* (Captain Gardiner), en route independently from the Tyne to Buenos Aires, was torpedoed in the Central Atlantic. Not one of her crew of forty-six was saved.

In April losses amongst the fleet of ships being managed by Ropners for the Ministry of Shipping escalated alarmingly. *Empire Moonrise* and *Empire Starlight* were both severely damaged by bombs – the latter eventually sinking – and *Empire Dryden* was torpedoed with the loss of her master and twenty-five of the crew.

The bravery of the crew of *Empire Starlight* during weeks of intensive air attacks on their ship is one of the epic stories of the war so far as Ropners is concerned. The story starts on 20 March 1942 when the convoy in which *Empire Starlight* was making the voyage to North Russia was scattered by bad weather. Half a dozen ships from the convoy made contact with each other the next day and thereafter this small group was subjected to daily attacks from the air, to appalling weather conditions and to heavy ice. The other five ships became jammed in the ice but were freed by *Empire Starlight* which sailed around them and cut them free. *Empire Starlight* managed to reach open water, but she lost touch with the other ships – two of which were later sunk – and reached Murmansk on her own on 27 March. From then onwards the ship and the port were subjected to heavy air attacks, often three or four in one day. *Empire Starlight* received more than one direct hit, but her crew continued to discharge her valuable cargo and her guns were responsible for the destruction of at least three enemy bombers. However, on 1 June she was hit by a stick of bombs on the port side and finally sunk.

For their bravery and resourcefulness during this hazardous period both the master, Captain Stein, and the chief engineer, Mr B. Morgan, were later awarded the OBE and the Lloyds' War Medal. The citation for the latter read as follows:

The ship, which was in convoy, reached a North Russian port undamaged in spite of heavy enemy air attacks. While in port she was again subjected to persistent attacks and sank. Throughout these fierce onslaughts, Captain Stein showed high courage and outstanding leadership. He did all that was possible to save his ship and obtained the discharge of a large part of her valuable cargo before she sank. Chief Engineer Morgan displayed calm courage and devotion to duty, especially when plugging leaks in the damaged engine-room under difficult and dangerous conditions.

April also saw the sinking of *Kirkpool* in the South Atlantic which was carried out by a German raider in a particularly ruthless manner. *Kirkpool* was making about 8 knots in a westerly direction on a pitch-black night, when the German ship opened fire at a distance of about two miles. At least one round of the first salvo was shrapnel and this burst just above the foremast. The raider then turned on her searchlight and sent a succession of salvoes into the steamer. A series of shells smashed into the engine room and then what was believed to be a torpedo exploded in number one hold. *Kirkpool* was now down by the head and had a heavy list, and though her engines were still running it was decided to abandon ship. As the boats were being lowered, however, the raider raked the boat deck with gunfire, destroying the boats and killing and wounding some of the crew. As the crew now made their way to the liferafts the raider continued to fire shrapnel, and several more men were killed. Eventually, those who were still alive managed to get away from their blazing ship, either on liferafts or on hatch-boards, and after half an hour the raider approached and picked up the survivors. This ferocious attack had cost the lives of sixteen of *Kirkpool*'s crew and later the master, Captain Kennington, and one other crew member were to die in a Japanese prisoner-of-war camp.

During the second half of the year the toll on ships managed by the firm continued to rise, with *Empire Rainbow* being torpedoed in July, without loss of life, and *Empire Arnold* going down on 4 August after being hit by a torpedo whilst on passage from the United States to the Middle East with a cargo of military stores. Nine men lost their lives and the master, Captain Tate, was taken prisoner on board the U-boat. Captain Downs, the master of *Reedpool*, was also taken prisoner by the U-boat which torpedoed his ship off the north coast of South America on 20 September.

In November *Daleby* was torpedoed in the North Atlantic, but all hands were saved; but when *Roxby* met the same fate a few days later she went down with thirty-four of her crew including the master, Captain Robinson.

With the sinking of *Lackenby* by a U-boat on 25 January 1943 the firm suffered another total disaster for she went down with all hands, forty-five in all. By now, however, the U-boat menace had been mastered and the tide of war had turned in favour of the Allies. The destruction of merchantmen dropped dramatically and the next Ropner losses did not occur until the invasion of Sicily in which several Ropner ships were involved, transporting vital supplies to the beachhead. On 6 July 1943 *Fort Pelly*, under the command of Captain Baty, left Alexandria with a cargo of cased petrol, vehicles, ammunition and stores for the Sicily forces. She arrived at Port Augusta on 18 July and started discharging her cargo. At 0335 on 20 July the ship was attacked by a dive bomber and sustained two direct hits and one near miss. One bomb exploded in the engine room and the other in number five hold. The whole of the amidships accommodation from the bridge aft, but not including the bridge, was destroyed, killing all the engineers. The bomb dropped aft demolished the entire end of the ship, including the crew's quarters. The master managed to escape from the lower bridge while it was under water but thirty-eight officers and men lost their lives.

Four days after *Fort Pelly* was sunk *Fishpool*, loaded with military stores, arrived at Syracuse harbour from Alexandria and dropped anchor in a berth to which Captain Churchill, the master of *Fort George*, had been directed.

Fishpool was one of those ships which had been dogged by bad luck throughout the war. On 14 November 1940 she was bombed while on her maiden voyage. A shower of incendiaries fell on her, killing all deck personnel, and in no time she became a blazing inferno. Two boatloads of survivors got away from her, but one of them, with fifteen men aboard, was never heard of again. Altogether twenty-six men, including the master, Captain Hill, lost their lives, but the ship was later salvaged and taken to the Clyde for repairs. In May 1941 she was lying at Barrow-in-Furness loading stores when the port was blitzed. A parachute mine landed on the quay right by the ship, causing her extensive damage and killing two of the crew.

Captain Churchill, on the other hand, considered himself a lucky man – 'born to be hanged', as he puts it. He had already survived no less than sixteen Atlantic voyages and the day before had distinguished himself by organizing the discharge of his cargo during a period of total confusion in the harbour, a piece of initiative for which he was later mentioned in dispatches. Now, he was about to have demonstrated to him just how lucky he was. He knew Captain Cole of *Fishpool* was relatively inexperienced, so he agreed to let him stay overnight while he found another berth nearby. At dawn the next morning the harbour was attacked by dive bombers and *Fishpool* received a direct hit amidships, starting a fire and causing casualties. Then she was hit twice more, and at 0600 the ammunition in her exploded and she was blown to pieces. Twenty-seven of the crew, including her master, lost their lives.

On 5 November 1943 *Bridgepool* was damaged by a mysterious explosion in the number one hold, and early the following year *Yearby* was damaged by a bomb attack. Apart from these incidents the two American liberty ships under Ropner management, *Sam Sylarna* and *Sam Suva*, were the only other casualties Ropners suffered during the rest of the war. *Sam Sylarna* was hit by an aerial torpedo aft on 4 August 1944, but was later beached off Benghazi. For his work in saving his ship and her valuable cargo, the master, Captain Hewison, was later awarded the O B E and the chief officer was commended.

Sam Suva was torpedoed on 29 September 1944 after leaving Archangel in convoy. The explosion killed three men, injured several others and caused a large fracture down both sides of the ship. The master, Captain Churchill, may have thought his luck had run out at last, but he and the remainder of the crew managed to get away before the ship broke in two and sank. Later Captain Churchill attended a naval inquiry into the sinking of his ship, as the convoy had been heavily escorted and any submarine in the area should have been detected. It transpired, however, that the last Ropner ship to be sunk in the war had been torpedoed by the first U-boat to use the new *Schnorkel* apparatus which enabled a submarine to stay submerged and undetected for long periods.

The devastation of the Ropner fleet between 1939 and 1944 was horrendous, but the war did not end without Ropner seamen again striking back at the enemy with satisfactory results. *Empire Grange* was off the Sicily beaches in December 1943 when she was attacked by a JU88 bomber flying about 100 feet above sea level. As it approached at about 200 m.p.h. the ship's starboard Oerlikons opened up and by the time the first pan of ammunition had been expended the plane was in flames. It dived steeply across the ship's bows and plunged into the sea.

In 1950, when Guy was president of the Chamber of Shipping, the Chamber's guest at its annual dinner was Field Marshal Viscount Montgomery of Alamein. After Guy had proposed a toast to the Fighting Forces Lord Montgomery replied by saying that the Merchant Navy had never failed him.

And so I say that victory was won in Hitler's war not only by the courage and skill of the Fighting Services, but also by the *quality* of the ships and men of the Merchant Navy – who transported us to our overseas bases and battlefronts, and maintained us there till the job was done. All this is quite apart from the fact that our country could never have survived either of the two world wars if our imports from overseas had not been maintained. And they *were* maintained in spite of the most determined attacks by the enemy to disrupt our sea communications.

10
Victory and Reconstruction

WHEN the war ended the Ropner Shipping Company only had *Yearby*, *Domby*, *Moorby* and *Danby* remaining afloat, while the Pool Shipping Company had only *Gullpool*, *Stagpool*, *Wearpool*, *Seapool*, *Cragpool*, *Bridgepool* and *Drakepool*. The last three were the oldest ships in the fleet and in 1947 they were sold, but in the meantime the fleet had been augmented by the purchase, under the government's Tonnage Replacement Scheme, of several 'Empire' (British-built) ships that had been managed by the firm during the war for the Ministry of Transport. These included *Empire Cabot*, renamed *Clearpool*; *Empire Sunbeam*, renamed *Swainby*; *Empire Clarion*, renamed *Cedarpool*; *Empire Tide*, renamed *Thirlby*; *Empire Irving*, renamed *Bellerby*; and *Empire Lionel*, renamed *Levenpool*. *Empire Mouflon*, renamed *Preston*, was also purchased for the newly formed Preston Shipping Company. Wholly owned by the company managing the two shipping fleets, Sir R. Ropner & Co. Ltd – which was, of course, still a private company at the time – the Preston Shipping Company only ever owned this one vessel. It was time-chartered for some years before being sold in 1951. Sir R. Ropner & Co. only ever owned one other ship, a cargo liner which was constructed at the Forges et Chantiers shipyard on the Gironde, but before she was launched Ropners withdrew from the trade she had been built for and she was sold to another company in 1957.

After acquiring these 'Empire' ships in 1945–46 the firm also time-chartered some 'Fort' (Canadian-built) and 'Ocean' (American-built) class ships as stop gaps, as well as continuing for a short time to manage several vessels for the Ministry of War Transport, including four German prize ships, *Kerston Miles*, *Adele Traber*, *Brigitte* and *Dalbek*. At the beginning of 1947 six 'Ocean' class ships were purchased from the Ministry of War Transport. *Ocean Vengeance* was renamed *Ingleby*; *Ocean Fame*, *Firby*; *Ocean Pride*, *Oakby*; *Ocean Valour*, *Heronspool*; *Ocean Vanity*, *Teespool*; and *Ocean Pilgrim*, *Pikepool*. In addition to these American-built ships, three others of the 'Sam' class were purchased direct from the United States government: *Samlistar*, which was renamed *Hurworth*; *Samdart*, renamed *Sedgepool*; and *Sam Tay*, renamed *Rudby*.

These wartime ships served the firm well for a number of years – the last was sold in 1962 – but they had been sometimes hurriedly constructed and occasionally were not as solid as they should have been. For instance, *Empire Mombasa*, one of the last to be built for the Ministry of War Transport and put under Ropner management, behaved in a most peculiar fashion when caught in a severe storm off Cape Wrath in February 1946. Her master, Captain Atkinson, reported to the firm that 'she shook violently from end to end like a wet dog'. The engine bedplate holding down bolts started to go, the main discharge pipe fractured, and all round the decks everything vibrated and worked to an unbelievable extent. Luckily, the weather moderated before assistance was required, and Captain Atkinson eventually made port safely without further incident.

This wartime tonnage had at one time looked like causing the same excess of carrying capacity which had caused the crash during the 1920s. In 1944 Robert Ropner had felt this problem loomed like 'a black cloud on the horizon' when he wrote an article about the difficulties facing the shipping industry after the war. 'It is most distressing,' he remarked, 'that a fleet which is now being hailed as a saviour of mankind is soon to become an embarrassment to British shipowners.'

Although these 'liberty' ships did indeed cause problems to British shipowners, if only because many of them were bought by foreign interests who then proceeded to challenge the dominance of the British merchant fleet, the worst of the 'boom and bust' times of the 1919–23 period, which Robert might well have thought would recur, was in fact avoided. Despite the very real difficulties confronting British shipping, the period between 1945 and 1957 was relatively prosperous. Exceptions were 1953 and 1954, but these were compensated for by high rates during the Korean War in 1951 and the Suez crisis of 1956. Nevertheless, lack of business in the hitherto thriving coal trade forced the closing of Ropners' Cardiff office in 1951.

The last half of the 1940s was a very busy one for the firm, and a period of change and reconstruction, Although derequisition was completed in 1946, cargo shipments, especially inwards, remained under government control for some years. For example, as late as 1952 the import of raw cotton was controlled and Ropners had to campaign hard to obtain a share of this market. A pamphlet released by the firm stated:

> Shipments of raw cotton from the United States to the Mersey are still Government controlled, and the Ropner Line – though Conference members, and though berthing first-class modern ships admirably equipped for the carriage and safe delivery of cotton – has not yet been allowed a share. The Lancashire cotton trade which was built by private enterprise has now been offered some measure of freedom insofar as the buying of cotton is concerned. Hence the directors of R. Ropner & Co. (Management) Ltd. have no hesitation in asking cotton shippers to show sympathy to private enterprise in another form – the Ropner Line.

Adjusting to the trading conditions of those times must have been hard and in fact many Ropner ships had to earn their money on the other side of the world, in Australia, where they were time-chartered. But just as it had been in 1918, the firm was lucky in 1945–46 in having all its directors and senior office staff, who had been scattered far and wide during the war, return to help it make the vital steps necessary to survive the new and more complex era that lay ahead.

In 1939 Leonard had been asked to join the Ministry of Supply. He had worked for it in various capacities, including the use of his expertise as a member of the Forestry Commission, but in 1941 the gravity of the war situation convinced him that he should enlist again and he rejoined the Army as a second lieutenant. Later, he commanded a light anti-aircraft regiment, and then a coast defence battery, and ended the war as a colonel with the British Military Government in Germany. He then returned to his parliamentary duties.

Guy was also away from the firm throughout the war. After starting as assistant director of the Board of Transport Control he became deputy director of the Ship Management Division and then the Minister's representative in Canada. He stayed in Canada two years before returning to Britain to take up the post of head of the Convoy Division. For this distinguished wartime career he was knighted in 1947.

Guy's eldest son, David, joined the Army in 1942 and was commissioned in the Royal Artillery in December 1943. In June 1944 he landed in Normandy shortly after D-Day and was posted to the 147 Essex Yeomanry Field Regiment (RA) with which he served for the rest of the war. He was demobilized as a captain in the middle of 1947 and joined the firm on 29 September of that year, the first of the fourth generation to do so. He became a director in 1953. In 1952 he was joined by his cousin, Jeremy, who had served in the Royal Navy. Jeremy became a director in 1958.

With his two elder brothers away, and Robert serving with a light anti-aircraft regiment, the burden of running the firm fell to Jock as *de facto* chairman, and he remained in such close touch with the office that, with his family, he lived right over it throughout the war. However, when the Ministry of Shipping started putting large numbers of ships under Ropner management it was decided by the Minister concerned that Jock needed assistance, and Robert, rather against his own wishes, was 'requisitioned' to help. He subsequently worked extensively with the Chamber of Shipping, becoming one of its representatives on the General Council of British Shipping (a different body to the present General Council which derived its name from it), eventually being made its vice-chairman and then chairman at the same time as he was vice-president and president of the Chamber of Shipping in 1956 and 1957 respectively. Throughout the war he was a member of the Deep Sea Tramp Negotiating Committee with the Ministry of War Transport, which involved him in liaison between the Chamber and the government over various wartime agreements, and over the derequisitioning of privately owned tonnage once hostilities ceased.

Both brothers were therefore heavily committed to government business, but they still found time to join the Home Guard, and early in 1943 were jointly responsible for capturing some German airmen who had parachuted from their disabled bomber. Once the war was over Robert remained involved with the Chamber of

Shipping. In 1947 he became chairman of the Tramp Standing Committee, an advisory body, and a member of the Transport Ship Licensing Committee. Jock's interests lay more with the Shipping Federation, the industry's employer/employee organization, for he wanted to attract the right kind of personnel to the merchant service. He was less involved than Robert in the official business of the industry, although towards the end of the war he did serve as the Ministry of War Transport's representative attached to the American Army in Brittany, and, later, as shipping adviser to SHAEF. His dedication in running the firm was recognized in 1948 when he was appointed an officer of the Order of Orange Nassau by Queen Wilhemina for his services in managing a number of Dutch vessels owned by the Halcyon Lijn during the war; and two years later he was also honoured by the French Government with the award of *Officier de l'Ordre du Mérite Maritime* for his wartime work in France.

Members of the staff who had served in the armed forces began returning to the firm by the end of 1945, though some were not able to rejoin until later. Mr Filby, Mr Handley and Mr Clouston, all of the head office, were demobilized from the Army, as were Mr Gidley of the London office and Mr Riddy and Mr Morgan of the Cardiff office; and Mr Dow and Mr Jackson of the head office were demobilized from the Navy, and Mr Symes of the London office from the RAF. In June 1946 a master, chief engineer and chief officer from the firm marched in London's Victory Parade as a tribute to the Ropner ships and men who had fought in the war. Ropners was also chosen to provide an apprentice as one of the standard bearers for the Merchant Navy contingent. The master taking part was Captain R. W. Thompson, who, as chief officer of *Empire Arnold*, had sailed an open boat with twenty-four survivors 500 miles to safety after the ship had been torpedoed in August 1942.

Once a nucleus of experienced staff had returned to head office it did not take the directors long to start operating a successful peacetime business once more. New offices were soon found and the move from the temporary accommodation in Sedgefield was made at the end of June 1946 to Greylands, a large house on Darlington's outskirts. This is still the head office today.

Moving away permanently from its roots at West Hartlepool and the sea did not lessen Ropners' commitment to shipping. On the contrary, as already mentioned, in 1946 the directors initiated a whole new side to the firm's business by starting a US Gulf of Mexico/UK cargo liner service, called the Ropner Line. The Ropner Line – or Gulf Line as it was often called within the firm – was run by Robert, with the help of Bill Gidley, while Jock remained in charge of tramp shipping operations. Leonard, of course, was fully occupied as a Member of Parliament and Guy, after his term as president of the Chamber of Shipping, devoted the majority of his time to Lloyds' Register of Shipping, of which he was a deputy chairman from 1950 to 1960.

The idea of the Ropner Line was suggested to Guy by Vassall Forrester, of Eggar, Forrester and Verner Ltd, an old-established firm of shipbrokers. Vassall Forrester had worked with Guy in Montreal during the war and later he set up a branch of his firm in New York. His suggestion was taken up enthusiastically by the four brothers – Jock asserts that tramp owners always have a hankering to run liners, as they are much cleaner and more glamorous than tramps! But there were a number of hard-nosed reasons too. The first, of course, was that it seemed as if such a line would be profitable if based on cargoes of grain out of the Gulf, topped up with other, better-paying, ones; while the outward voyage from Liverpool, Dublin, Manchester and London could carry mixed cargoes, ranging from cars and whisky to machinery and cement. The passenger side started in a very modest way – Ropners had always carried a passenger or two, and during the 1930s their fares had sometimes made the difference between a voyage being profitable or not – but the later ships carried twelve passengers in considerable luxury and proved very popular.

Apart from the obvious necessity of making such a venture profitable the directors were motivated by the need to attract the best type of sea-going personnel and were keen that the old ditty

Ashes to ashes and dust to dust,
If Cunard won't have you then Ropners must

should no longer necessarily apply. There was, however, a very good reason why the best officers were not attracted to a tramp company: wages on tramp steamers were inflexible, but on liners owners could pay whatever they felt they could afford. The regularity of a line was also a bonus for sea-going personnel whose families naturally liked to know when they would be home, a luxury rarely enjoyed by those in the tramp trade. The new line was also an attraction to the shore-based staff for it became a policy of the firm that as many wives as possible should be allowed to accompany their husbands on the run so long as it did not interfere with the efficient administration of the firm or the ships.

After some negotiation Ropners became an associate member of the North Atlantic Liner Conference in order to trade with the United States out of the UK, and it also joined the two American conferences, the Gulf of Mexico/UK and the Gulf of Mexico/Continent, thus enabling it to have a share in the export of the American materials like carbon black, cotton and sulphur. Brown Jenkinson were appointed London loading brokers and Bahr, Behrend the Mersey loading brokers. Eggar, Forrester and Verner became the firm's New York general representatives, with Boyd Weir and Sewell the New York cargo forwarding brokers; the Strachan Shipping Company was its shipping agent in the various Gulf ports except Miami where Shaw Brothers were appointed.

The line was inaugurated on 28 September 1946 when *Moorby*, one of the two motor vessels built in the 1930s, sailed from Hull and then loaded at New Orleans and Houston for London and Bremen. Shortly afterwards, she was joined on the run by *Teespool*, an ex-'Ocean' class ship, and at the height of the line's popularity the firm had four vessels employed on it. At first there was no shortage of cargo, despite government restrictions, as Marshall Aid to Europe was in full swing. But later, as competition from both American and British lines increased – and cargoes like raw cotton and carbon black decreased because of technological changes – it became more difficult, and eventually impossible, to make ends meet.

Nevertheless, the first postwar ships built for the firm were constructed for the Gulf Line. *Daleby(3)*, a 445-foot, 5000-ton gross motor ship, went into service in May 1950, and her sister ship, *Deerpool(2)*, three months later. Both were built by Sir James Laing and Sons Ltd of Sunderland and were powered by a two-stroke-cycle, single-acting Doxford oil engine of the latest design, which gave them a designed maximum speed of 12½ knots – though this was easily exceeded by *Daleby* during her trials.

The earlier ships on the Gulf Line run had only had room for one or two passengers, but both the new ships could take a dozen in total comfort, the accommodation consisting of five double cabins with adjoining bathrooms and the owners' suite which cost slightly more; a dining room; a spacious lounge; and even a full-sized cocktail bar. The crew were equally well provided for, each man having his own cabin, an almost unheard of luxury in those days. *The Times* called *Daleby* a miniature Atlantic liner. 'Externally,' wrote the paper's shipping correspondent, 'the *Daleby* looks a smart cargo liner with a green hull [the new colour adopted by the firm a few years previously], white band and white upper works, and green funnel. Internally the fittings of the passenger accommodation, with white-painted corridors, well-furnished cabins, each with baths or showers, dining saloon, lounge, writing room, and smoking room and bar, remind the visitor of the equipment of much larger transatlantic passenger liners.'

The relief of getting *Daleby* into the water was very evident from the firm's newsletter, *Ropner Record*:

> Hardly a single department in the office but is relieved that this addition to the fleet is at last in commission. The Superintendents have put new ships in the water before today, but never one with problems like this. The Stores Department took new ships in their stride till this one came along. Personnel and Passenger Departments have been having sleepless nights for months. And over all, the Directors and Managers – considering, rejecting, approving, amending, suggesting, worrying, and wondering.

But there was enthusiasm too for the new ship, for with her lay the future aspirations of the directors and staff alike. 'And now she IS. Half a million pounds' worth of her. Fashioned and furnished, painted and petted, moulded and manned, nursed and nurtured, for better or worse. The pride of the fleet. The dream come true.'

At her launching, however, Jock had to strike a cautionary note amidst all the enthusiasm. The government, he said in his speech, seemed to take almost a pleasure in placing industrialists in a position where they could not see more than a few weeks or days ahead. Taxation was a very heavy burden and conditions generally were uncertain. Freight rates had been good, but now if a ship went to Australia in ballast she lost around £12,000, and around £7000 if she went to the Plate. 'I am referring in these cases,' he said, 'to a fairly modern 9000-ton oil-burning cargo vessel. The prospects, therefore, for shipowners today, and shortly for shipbuilders, are not so good.'

As an indication of how tramp shipping flourished – or, rather, failed to – during those postwar years one has only to look at, first, the valuation put on the Ropner fleet between 1948 and 1949, and, second, the size of the fleet itself. The valuation of the oldest ship in the fleet, *Gullpool*, built in 1928, was £102,600 in August 1948, but just over a year later, in October 1949, this figure had dropped to £50,000. The firm's newest and biggest vessel, *Rudby*, 10,559 tons dw and built in 1944, was valued at £153,000 in August 1948 and at £140,000 in October 1949.

If these valuations are compared with what happened to the value of ships after the First World War the similarities are plain to see; but if one compares the sizes of the fleet any similarity with what happened in the 1920s ceases, for even in the worst of those years the number of Ropner ships did not contract as they started to do from 1950 onwards. In that year three ships were sold, with only two launched, while in the following four years five were sold and two launched. At the end of this time the firm was only running the four new motor ships for the Gulf Line, *Somersby* and *Swiftpool* having been launched in 1954, plus the wartime tonnage bought under the government's Tonnage Replacement Scheme. These were all coal-burners and a programme was started to convert them to burning oil.

Ropners, though, was not alone in running a fleet of mostly wartime tonnage which was shrinking in numbers annually. As Robert pointed out in 1952 at the annual meeting of the Chamber of Shipping's Deep Sea Tramp Section, which he chaired, the amount of British tramp tonnage had dropped from 3.4 million tons gross in 1930 to 3 million in 1950 and to 2.8 million in 1951, though liner tonnage had remained more or less constant throughout this same period. By 1952 the decline had accelerated, with tramp tonnage being reduced to 2.4 million tons gross, a drop as large as that between 1939 and 1950.

The greatest single cause for this decline was not the freight rates, but the high level of taxation which made it impossible to set aside sufficient funds for replacement tonnage. At the launching of *Swiftpool* Robert returned to these problems by pointing out that the new ship had cost twelve times the amount spent on constructing her predecessor in 1929 and by attacking a government Minister's recent complacent statement that British tonnage was as great as it had been before the war. 'This is one of those very dangerous half-truths,' Robert remarked, 'that are more dangerous possibly than an actual falsehood'; that the truth of the matter was that the 12.3 million tons gross of dry cargo shipping on the UK register in September 1939 had fallen to 10.9 million tons in June 1953, the difference being made up by the increase in tanker tonnage. Furthermore, he added that nearly 40 per cent of the British dry cargo ships afloat in 1954 was built in the war and that these vessels would need replacing within the next six years at an estimated cost of between £450 and £500 million.

The postwar problems of the British shipping industry had, in fact, begun to be voiced some years earlier. Guy, who in 1949 had been elected vice-president of the Chamber of Shipping, succeeding to the presidency in 1950, stated in his presidential address that 'there is still no power in this regimented world to force people to buy something they do not want and cannot afford, and ways and means must therefore be found to enable builders to offer tonnage to owners at prices which will appeal to them. Boom prices during a slump do not make sense.' He also pointed out that while the British Government gave no help to British shipowners, their competitors abroad were 'helped on their way by favourable tax remissions, State and municipal loans, equalizing subsidies, reservation of certain classes of cargo in certain proportions to the national flag, currency restrictions and, in some cases, open flag discrimination. In the international field, as in any other, it is impossible to fight modern armour with a wooden sword.'

Another real cause for anxiety was the strikes that plagued the postwar years. The dockers, the miners, the railwaymen, to mention only some, seemed to take it in turns to go slow or walk out, with appalling results for those businessmen trying to earn valuable dollar currency. In 1955 Jock wrote:

> Our experience at UK ports of discharge has been disastrous. Commencing with the London dock strike, which in itself resulted in a loss of many thousands of pounds, some of our subsequent discharging turns have varied only in so far as they have been either very bad or so prolonged as to be hardly credible, for instance:
>
> Ship 'A' in the Mersey (with part cargo)

2 days at the Bar
11 days at waiting berth
10 days discharging 5,580 tons of cargo
or ship 'B' also in the Mersey (with part cargo)
3 days at the bar
2 days waiting for labour
14 days discharging 5,345 tons of cargo
or ship 'C'
29 days discharging at Liverpool, Manchester, and Glasgow (Glasgow 9 days for 1,345 tons)

If these ships had discharged all their cargo totalling 22,500 tons at North Continental ports they would have saved about 20 days each or 60 days in all representing a reduction in operating costs of some £20,000 or about 18/- per ton on the cargo carried. Obviously a switch to Continental discharging ports is in our minds.

Each of the four new motor vessels engaged in the liner Service performs one round voyage fewer per year than scheduled solely on account of port delays. They run late for their commitments and cause embarrassment and loss to shippers and receivers.

There is a growing desire on the part of those shipowners who are not irretrievably committed to UK ports to avoid them at all costs.

But perhaps the greatest single financial problem that beset the firm in the immediate postwar years was caused by the death of William on 17 March 1947, aged eighty-two.

For over forty years William had run the firm, first with the help of his brother John and then aided by his four sons. Although he had more or less retired during the war years he was always ready to be consulted and would still occasionally appear at the office. During the 1920s and early 1930s, his most active years as senior partner, he had shown a commitment to the shipping industry which few could rival, but, as with his father before him, his interests ranged far beyond his business commitments. For more than thirty years he was president of the Hartlepools' Crippled Children's League and in 1913 he bought and furnished a large house at Elwick so that crippled children could be brought there to enjoy a holiday each year. In 1925 he proposed a scheme for opening private gardens to the public, which he called Garden Sunday and publicized the idea through the letters column of *The Times*. An outstandingly generous gesture was when he made a donation towards saving the voluntary hospitals in London. 'To all who understand the needs of the voluntary hospitals of London,' wrote a leader writer in *The Times* of 2 October 1922, 'we commend today the letter, and the example therein, by Mr William Ropner of West Hartlepool, who sends us a cheque for £10,000, to be handed over to the Treasurer of the Hospitals of London Combined Appeal. It is an exceedingly handsome gift, and it comes at a most appropriate moment.' The appeal was headed by the Prince of Wales and the next day the paper reprinted a letter from the Prince to William thanking him for his contribution.

Apart from his business and charitable interests, William was a county magistrate for many years and was a member of the Hartlepool Port and Harbour Commission from 1904 to 1942, being chairman from 1925 to 1939.

William's death brought with it such heavy estate duties that his four sons had very little alternative but to constitute a holding company and to seek a quotation on the stock exchange as a public company in order to raise sufficient capital to remain in business on a profitable basis. As a first step a firm of London accountants was asked to recommend the basis of exchange between shares in the two shipping companies and those of the new holding company, to be known as Ropner Holdings Ltd. The accountants recommended that for each £1 share in the Pool Shipping Company a shareholder should receive a £1 share in the new holding company plus a distribution in cash at the rate of 3s 10d per share out of the capital reserve, and that for every three shares of 13s 4d in the Ropner Shipping Company a shareholder should receive two £1 shares in the new holding company. This was agreed to by the shareholders and on 6 December 1948 Ropner Holdings Ltd was registered to acquire the shares of the two shipping companies. The new company had a registered capital of £1,759,606 and had the same directors as the managing company, Sir R. Ropner & Co. Ltd, which remained a private company having a management agreement with the public company. Two years later the management company's name was changed to Sir R. Ropner & Co. (Management) Ltd.

11
Diversification

In the 1952 New Year Honours List a baronetcy was conferred on Leonard for his political services as a Member of Parliament for twenty-six years, a time during which he had immersed himself in a whole variety of political activities. However, this did not stop him from remaining a staunch and formidable supporter of the shipping industry for whose interests he must have fought on numerous committees. 'His manner doesn't change,' remarked a colleague when Leonard was battling for something in committee. 'He is tremendously polite – but it's like trying to shift a rock.'

But even Leonard's rocklike tenacity made little headway against a government which imposed crippling taxation, which refused to act against fierce overseas competition and which seemed incapable of avoiding the long series of damaging strikes that so scarred the industry. As a result, by 1959 the UK-owned deep-sea tramp fleet had been reduced by about 1 million tons compared with the prewar fleet, although the world's tramp tonnage had more than doubled during the same period. Inevitably, Ropners was as much a victim of these factors as other shipowners and, although at the launching of its newest cargo liner, *Somersby*, in 1954, Leonard was able to say that cargo bookings for the Gulf Line were increasing fast, three years later Jock was having to announce to the shareholders that the line was to close, crushed by a series of damaging strikes and by competition from powerful overseas shipping lines. This must have been a sad blow to the directors, but while the Gulf Line was at the height of its success the decision had been made to try another sector of shipping new to Ropners – tankers – and this, though limited in scope, had a much happier outcome.

The success of Ropners' entry into the oil freight market was not because the firm went into it, as some others did, in a big way. On the contrary, one of the most successful aspects of this short-lived diversification was that the directors were not tempted – or rather resisted the temptation – to go on building to take advantage of the buoyant market that existed during the first half of the 1950s. Insteady, they launched only two tankers, the 18,000-ton dw *Thornaby*, in 1953, and the 21,000-ton dw *Thirlby*, in 1958. A third was contracted for, to be built in a shipyard at Le Trait on the River Seine, but the contract was later cancelled before construction began. The cancellation proved to be expensive, but was doubtless considerably cheaper than having a huge investment like a tanker on the books in a market which, by 1958, was as flat as a pancake. As Robert pointed out at *Thirlby*'s launch, there had been only 15 million gross tons of tankers in 1948, whereas nine years later there was 32 million gross tons. Inevitably, tankers began being tied up, so that by the time *Thirlby* was launched 3 million gross tons world wide was idle and new tankers often went straight from the shipyard to their laying-up berths.

The success of trading *Thornaby* and *Thirlby* lay in the fact that both were time-chartered and not kept in the spot market, making them forerunners of how the modern Ropner fleet is run. *Thornaby* was time-chartered for five years initially to BP – at that time the longest period Ropners had ever chartered one of their ships – and *Thirlby* was bareboat-chartered to Shell, with the management retained by the firm. This latter charter ultimately lasted twenty-three years.

Within the parameters of shipping another postwar endeavour was the expansion of the family-owned Elton Stores. Originally just the firm's ships' stores department, of which the canvas loft in Mainsforth Terrace was a part, Elton Stores was formed in 1947 and managed by the stores superintendent, Mr O'Dair. Over the years it expanded considerably and apart from providing ships stores to the fleet – and to other ships – it became a chandlery and sold or leased out all kinds of canvas articles like lorry covers, tents and marquees. It did agency work, contracted for supplying stevedoring services, and operated a company bond at its warehouse at Houndgate. And when the number of ships had dwindled to such an extent that its original function was no longer viable on its own, it even branched out into providing food to hotels, rented out caravans and sold shotgun cartridges. At one time it owned a ships' chandlery business in Southampton, but the age of specialization overtook it eventually and it ceased to remain profitable. In April 1966 its name was changed to Mainsforth Investments Ltd, which is still a family concern for investment purposes. New Elton Stores, a subsidiary of Ropner Holdings, was incorporated in May 1966 to carry on the business of supplying stores, but though it is still in existence it ceased trading in 1969.

In 1955 Percy Dyer, who had become Ropner Holdings first non-family director in 1951, died. In the prewar days Percy had fixed many Ropner ships with coal cargoes from the northeast coalfields through Common Brothers chartering office in Newcastle. He knew the collieries and the type of coal they produced so intimately that he could order exactly the right mixture for the bunkers of each ship. A present family director of the firm wrote:

> Percy was, and will remain always in memory, the complete shipping man. He fulfilled many roles in the company during his time but for the years previous to his death he was director in charge of insurance and claims. Nothing could happen that Percy had not already experienced and he knew exactly how to deal with any problem whenever, or however, it arose. Practical as he was, Percy also had a streak of superstition in his nature; if a ship of a certain name had had a succession of unfortunate experiences in the 1880s for example, it would be futile to suggest to him that that name should be used again for a new ship in the 1950s.

When Percy died his job of dealing with the marine insurance and maritime law side of the business was taken over by his assistant, George Filby, who had joined in 1932. However, with the number of ships rapidly decreasing – in 1960 the fleet had shrunk to twelve, with none on order – George soon found himself with a dwindling workload. Having a basic fund of insurance knowledge, he suggested to Jock that it might be a good idea if Ropners started a general broking agency. Jock gave his blessing and after George had had several helpful conversations with Henry Head Ltd, Ropners' main insurance brokers at Lloyds, the Ropner Insurance Agency was formed in 1957. The agency's first customer was a local market gardener – who still insures through Ropners – and later several broking companies in Leeds and Tees-side were bought up and amalgamated, in 1960, into Ropner Insurance Brokers. In George Filby's words, this never really hit the big time, but later it had an important impact on the directors when further expansion into insurance was being considered.

While these efforts were being made postwar to find new sources of profit within the firm the directors were also investing in a small way in outside ventures.

Leonard had made his first flight well before the First World War. By the 1930s he had obtained a pilot's license and from his parliamentary speeches during this period it is obvious that he had a great interest in air transport. So when, in the spring of 1944, two judges in the Chancery Division confirmed the legality of a change in the objects of the Pool and the Ropner shipping companies to enable them to carry on the business of transport by air as well as by sea, it is reasonable to assume that Leonard was one of the driving forces behind this farsighted move. However, as it was still wartime nothing could be planned at that time, but by making the changes then the companies were ready to participate in whatever opportunities arose once hostilities ceased. These came fairly swiftly for, by the autumn of 1945, Robert was chairman of a committee set up by thirty-seven shipping companies to try and form an air charter company to be called Shipping Airlines Ltd. The idea was to cover cargo routes to and from the Continent, with aircraft being offered for charter in the same way that cargo ships were available in the freight market. The company was never formed, but out of this idea sprang Ropners' connection with Chartair Ltd, an air charter company formed by a small group of shipowners, and others, in 1946.

One of the original shareholders in Chartair was Lambert Brothers Ltd, the Lloyds insurance brokers, which on occasion acted for Ropners in the insurance market and which had shipping interests themselves. George Talbot Willcox, who was married to William Ropner's only daughter, Winsome, was a director of Lamberts. In 1914 he had joined the Highland Light Infantry and had served at Gallipoli. After transferring to the Royal Flying Corps, he had served on the Western Front for the last two years of the war. At the start of the Second World War he joined the RAF and served with Fighter Command at Stanmore. He saw the potential of Chartair and encouraged the Ropner directors to take a small shareholding in the new company. By employing both the Pool and Ropner shipping companies to buy shares, the four brothers acquired double the number allotted to the other shipping shareholders – 13,333 in total, about 10 per cent of the equity. Rarely has such a comparatively minor investment had such a profound effect on a company as well established and as secure as Ropners.

Chartair's headquarters were at Hanwell but, as there were no customs facilities there, its first two aircraft, a war-surplus Airspeed Consul and a De Havilland Rapide, were operated from Croydon. In February 1947 Airtech Ltd, a subsidiary of Chartair, was formed to service Chartair's aircraft. It was incorporated as a private company with an authorized share capital of £25,000, which was increased to £50,000 on 1 May 1947. It commenced business on a 300-acre airfield at Haddenham, with the airfield's prewar owners as one of its initial shareholders.

During its first year Airtech recruited personnel to handle the repair and maintenance of several types of aircraft, up to and including the four-engined Halifaxes, and by the end of 1948 it was employing 350 people. One of its earliest employees was Sydney Codling, now chairman of Airtech Ltd, who joined as chief inspector a month after the company had been formed. 'I think the shareholders saw Chartair as a worldwide chartering company,' he said, 'a sort of tramp fleet in the air', a visionary project indeed but one which, through government legislation if nothing else, was doomed to failure.

Initially, though, Chartair expanded its air fleet, owning a number of Airspeed Consuls and Procters, two Rapides and, later, some civilian versions of the Halifax, called the Halton. But because it was not properly controlled or perhaps simply because cargo was hard to come by, the company did not prosper. The Berlin Airlift which started in 1948 and ran for about a year probably saved it from bankruptcy but what other business came its way was often unusual. On one occasion, for instance, a Humber car was swapped for a load of Spanish fruit as cars were even more difficult to come by in Spain than fresh oranges in Britain. Sydney Codling remembers the car being slung beneath a Halton and flown out dangling under its fuselage! On another, two Beaufighters owned by Chartair were flown out of the country under the guise of having a film made about them. As they had cost Chartair £1000 each and had been sold for £25,000 each to the Israeli Government to boost its country's air defences it proved to be a profitable deal. However, such favourable business undertakings were rare and once the government implemented its declared policy of concentrating all civil aviation activities on the two nationalized airlines Chartair ceased to trade, though it remained in existence until the early 1960s.

Airtech, on the other hand, flourished. Sydney Codling would buy government-surplus aircraft and convert them for civilian use. Once they had been made airworthy they would be sold to Chartair, or to an associate airline, British-American Air Services, which merged with Chartair in 1947, or to other operators. Later, Airtech became approved converters of the Halifax into the civilian Halton and a number of these were sold to firms like Eagle Aviation and Freddie Laker's Aviation Traders. When the Berlin Airlift started Airtech was one of the very few companies capable of servicing and repairing large four-engined planes. As a result of this expertise the company was called upon to fulfil many urgent requirements. One of the most exacting was installing a sophisticated navigational radar, REBECCA, and a high-frequency radio called BABS with which aircraft flying into Berlin were monitored along the flightpath and onto the airfields.

One of the main aims of the Berlin Airlift was to supply the city with diesel oil. In order to do this, a large number of aircraft were modified by Airtech to carry 1500-gallon diesel fuel tanks in the bomb bays. The tanks were acquired from various surplus dumps around the country and refurbished before being fitted complete with new streamline fairings.

When the Airlift ended and the servicing of the privately owned freight carriers dwindled, the advanced radio and electrical servicing department, and the workshops set up for the overhaul and repair of hydraulic equipment, engines and instruments stood Airtech in good stead for finding new business. For example, the British South American Airlines Corporation contracted it to design, build and install a special pannier to be fitted to a Lincoln aircraft so that spare engines could be transported in it to various parts of the world where the Corporation operated.

Despite the drop in demand the servicing of aircraft was still continued, and as it was done regardless of cost Airtech now began to lose money. Lamberts sent in their group accountant and shortly afterwards there was a management shake-up. George Talbot Willcox became the new Airtech chairman with Sydney Codling as his general manager, and these two, plus company secretary Jack Matthews and aviation expert Bob Mayo, formed a management committee. The servicing of aircraft ceased, and, because so many of the staff were ex-RAF personnel, including Sydney Codling, a close working relationship began with the RAF which over the years was to prove very fruitful. In 1950 contracts were obtained for the repair and overhaul of American radio equipment of the type fitted to Dakotas and other aircraft of Transport Command, and servicing contracts were also won for radio transmitters/receivers and for radio compasses. Eventually, some 300 individual units of equipment were being routed through the workshops for repair and overhaul, and extensive facilities had to be installed to cope with what, in those days, were considered to be very high-powered starter generators, actuators and other heavy-duty electrical equipment. Later, these facilities enabled Airtech to win the contract to repair all the electrical equipment fitted to the Royal Canadian Air Force Sabre jets operating in Europe, work which took it into the transistor age.

Work also started during the early 1950s on the development and construction of a revolutionary helicopter which involved the use of magnesium alloy for the first time in airframe construction. Sadly, this project came to nothing – one of Airtech's few failures – and the machine is now on permanent display at the Cranfield Aeronautical College.

On the engineering and mechanical side Airtech also took on a number of subcontracts, including the manufacture of aircraft components for Hunting Percival which eventually led to Airtech building the whole nose of the Percival Prince, from the pilot's seat forward, including the installation of all the flying instrumentation and electrics. Other work included a contract with Alvis to manufacture the gun turret of their troop carrier and the design and construction of a tilt platform at the Ministry of Defence's fighting vehicle research establishment at Chobham.

Attempts to interest the Ministry of Defence in Airtech's expertise in the field of aircraft radio installation did not produce any contracts, but when one of the Ministry's main contractors suffered a fire it was found that extra capacity was urgently needed for the installation of radio equipment in R A F vehicles, and Airtech promptly stepped into the breach. However, it was soon found that the vehicles supplied were unsuitable to have such complex equipment fitted in them and so Airtech began to develop a small container for the communications equipment which would fit into a Britannia aircraft. This proved to be something of a breakthrough and eventually a whole range of these 'Aircon' containers, manufactured in steel, light alloy and plastic, all of which offered a high degree of mobility and air portability for highly delicate electronic equipment, were available to the Ministry of Defence, overseas governments and civil aviation authorities. It was this unique experience in systems engineering which ultimately led to Airtech being currently involved in the Army's largest communications project ever.

Airtech's success in obtaining these servicing and equipment contracts meant that it was overly dependent on the Ministry of Defence and so efforts were made to introduce new products. Arrangements were made to manufacture under license from two French companies containers and lifting equipment, and the Gichner Mobile System under license from the United States. Then in November 1957 an exclusive licence agreement was entered into to manufacture and sell hose couplings, an idea of German origin which Sydney Codling had picked up through a business colleague. Initial design problems diverted what had originally been an idea for industrial use into a plastic connector for garden hoses. After a modest first season of sales, a spray nozzle was added to the range and in November 1959 Hozelock Ltd was incorporated with an authorized share capital of £50,000, of which £1000 was issued and subscribed for in cash by the shareholders of Airtech. Sydney Codling went to the United States several times to try and sell this new product and instead ended up importing garden sprinklers from there to add to the Hozelock range. These sold well and within a short space of time Hozelock was manufacturing its own. In the first four years of trading (1960–64) Hozelock's gross profits rose from £46,661 to £110,845.

An investment was also made in Soundcraft Magnetics Ltd which was incorporated in May 1961. The idea of this company, which, with two exceptions, had the same shareholders as Airtech, was to import and distribute a range of magnetic tape and film but it was never profitable and was wound up a few years later. Much more successful was the licence agreement entered into with two Americans, cousins, Mr Pete and Mr Milton Green, who after the war had started a company called the Plumbium Manufacturing Corporation which manufactured wheel balance weights. Sydney Codling heard that they wished to set up a joint venture company in Britain to produce and sell their product and in June 1962 Airvert Ltd – 'Air' from Airtech, 'vert' meaning green – was incorporated with an authorized share capital of £15,000 divided into 7650 'A' shares of £1 each and 7350 'B' shares of £1 each. Airtech subscribed in full for the 'A', and the 'B' shares were taken up by the Greens. Gross profit in the last six months of 1962 was £3315, and this increased to £19,929 in 1963, the first complete year of trading.

On 24 October 1961 Airtech acquired the undertaking of Chartair Ltd, including the airfield at Haddenham which until then had been leased from Chartair. In consequence the authorized share capital was increased to £250,000, the issued share capital being £221,485. As a result of purchasing some of these shares, and by buying from other shareholders who had dropped out, by the end of 1963 Ropners had about a 46 per cent holding in the company spread between the two shipping companies and the management company. The other major shareholder was Airtech's chairman Sir Eric Ohlsen, his brother and the Ohlsen Steamship Company, while Lambert Brothers Ltd and D. Salisbury Green, the only other remaining original shareholders, had minority holdings.

Ropners' increased percentage in Airtech did not come about as a matter of policy; rather it was that the four Ropner brothers simply felt the concern worth their continuing support. The profits were modest, but then, compared with the construction of a modern cargo ship, so was the investment. However, the firm's greater financial involvement in Airtech meant another Ropner director was needed to join Robert, Airtech's vice-chairman. So Robert's eldest son, Bruce, who had joined the firm in January 1954 after completing his National Service in the Welsh Guards and who had been a director of Ropner Holdings since January 1960, was elected to the Airtech board in February 1962. He remembers going to one of his first monthly board meetings, regularly held at the Dorchester Hotel, with a special question from his uncle Jock who wanted to know why the meetings were always held at such an expensive venue. When the agenda had been completed Sir Eric asked if there was anything else which should be discussed. Why, asked Airtech's newest director dutifully, were the board meetings held at such a costly hotel as the Dorchester? 'Because it's cheaper than the Savoy,' Sir Eric replied crisply. 'Any other business?'

Like Airtech, the firm's investment in its other postwar outside interest, Eggar, Forrester and Verner, really came about as much by chance as through any calculated policy of the Ropner board. It sprang, as had the idea for the Gulf Line, out of the friendship between Guy and Vassall Forrester. Besides being shipbrokers and running an import–export business, Eggar, Forrester also ran a chartering agency and the four brothers felt that by holding a majority interest in it they could create some competitiveness with their own London shipbroking and chartering branch without diverting badly needed profits to outside interests. The arrangement worked well for a number of years, with the Ropner family interest – the shares had been acquired by Ropner (London), which, like the shipping management company, was still privately owned – being represented on the board by Guy and Jock. Then, in 1960, the chairman, Norman Eggar died, which meant a readjustment in the financial ownership. George Talbot Willcox's son, Peter, who had been with Eggar, Forrester since 1948, became managing director of the group, but as he needed someone to sort out the export trading side of the business he organized a merger the following year with the British Overseas Engineering Credit Company (BOECC) run by an old friend, Simon Kimmins. Hambro, Rothschilds and Taylor, Woodrow each took a 7 per cent shareholding, while Ropner (London) retained its 51 per cent, and Peter and Simon became joint managing directors under the chairmanship of Jock. Ropners' association with Rothschilds dates from this period.

The last years of the 1950s must have been very busy ones for the brothers, especially for Robert. Not only was he involved with the firm – after William died all four brothers became joint managing directors – but he sat on the board of Airtech, was chairman of the North of England Protection and Indemnity Associations in 1956, and maintained his interest in the Chamber of Shipping where he was chairman of the Deep Sea Tramp Section between 1951 and 1953, before going on to be elected vice-president of the Chamber in 1956 and then president the following year.

'That restless and irrepressible ball of fire,' was the retiring president's description of Robert when he took up the presidency in 1957. 'He is terrific, as you will discover.' Certainly Robert threw himself into his new job with great energy, and the newspaper clippings of his year in office reveal him as a much travelled and constant campaigner on behalf of the shipping industry. In radio broadcasts and television interviews as well as in his numerous speeches – always the lot of the Chamber's president – he warned that the problems facing the industry were extremely serious ones. He was particularly outspoken about the increasing practise of using flags of convenience and clashed in the correspondence column of *The Times* with one of their arch proponents, Stavros Niarchos. He fought long and hard for a fairer deal from the government for the industry, and when it was proposed to impose a 3 per cent levy on the use of the Suez Canal to pay for the cost of clearing it after the 1956 war he led a delegation to 10 Downing Street to talk to the Prime Minister. Soon after he relinquished the presidency he was knighted for his services to shipping.

The political and financial hazards facing British shipping which preoccupied Robert during his year as president of the Chamber of Shipping were very real ones indeed. Because of them the industry was less able to survive the shipping slump of the early 1960s, and many shipowners were forced to cease trading. Ropners was not one of them, but the severity of the slump did bring about within the firm a whole new phase of development, one which was eventually to cause the most fundamental change in its history.

12
The Modern Conglomerate

In the years following the Second World War the non-family directors began to play an increasingly important role.

'In the course of recent history the names of Percy Dyer, William Wiley, Charles Ringwood and Bill Gidley are remembered by the present generation of family directors with particular gratitude and affection.'

The role of Percy Dyer has been mentioned earlier. Of an equally practical nature – but perhaps more severely so – was William Wiley Jr (although the present generation of the family could not imagine anybody more senior than he), who served the company from 1915 to 1965, latterly as director in charge of fleet operations under Jock. Every business morning he would converse with the senior broker in London at 12.00 precisely. One suspects that he would still have done so if the Baltic Exchange had been destroyed by an earthquake and the broker had had to speak from a bed in hospital. Having finished his conversation Will would make his calculations; there were no desktop calculators in those days but Will would most probably not have bothered to use one even if there had been, his own brain was just as accurate. His conclusions would then be discussed with Jock and the necessary instructions relayed to London. A large filing cabinet in Will's room contained all the charters of all the ships for many years back but Will's own mind was almost equally commodious and there were few clauses, terms or conditions with which he was not familiar.

For many years after the war Bill Gidley assisted Will Wiley in the chartering and operations department. He had an expert knowledge of the workings of the Baltic Exchange since he had been originally employed as a broker there in 1930, and worked on the Exchange up to the time he joined the Rifle Brigade at the beginning of the war.

Five years rigorous (and at time extremely dangerous) war service in North Africa and Italy in a crack regiment left its mark on Bill. At times of stress or urgency in the office his normal progress would be at the double; he had the soldier's knack of being able to scent trouble before it came, and many was the occasion when Bill's canny foresight averted problems or ensured that a contingency plan was drawn up in good time.

Besides assisting Will Wiley until his own time came to take his place Bill was responsible under Robert for liner operations. Like everything he did he did this with great efficiency and almost missionary-like zeal. At the same time he was charged with keeping an eye on the then-youngest generation of the family who were receiving their initiation into the world of shipping, and they feel that they have good reasons to be grateful to him for what they learned. Bill liked to indulge his soldier's penchant for 'bellyaching', and it often seemed to him that dark and alien forces were at work to ensure that competitors of the Ropner Line got more high-paying cargo than Ropners got. No one tried harder to see that they didn't. In later years, when his responsibilities included those of office manager, it was his custom to stand each morning at a window overlooking the staff car park. Anyone whose car had not arrived by the requisite time would later have to explain the reason, and Bill (an ex-RSM) was a difficult man to persuade.

Charles Ringwood joined the company at the office in Mainsforth Terrace, West Hartlepool, in 1916, at the age of fifteen. At that time he was the new office boy responsible only for the rather menial fetch and carry duties which that post entailed at the time. Later, however, he was to become the trusted confidant of three generations of the family, upon whose history and business endeavours he was the supreme authority, and to whose interest he tirelessly and selflessly devoted his entire working life.

From the 1930s until his retirement (after sixty years' service) in 1976 nothing of significance was decided or done before Charles had been consulted about it and approved it. Very often it would be Charles who actually did it. Although by nature not in the least thrusting or given to interference, he was the sort of man who invited trust by his thoughtful and responsive manner and his dignified unflappability. Any particularly delicate matter, or one which needed handling with the consummate diplomacy which was natural to Charles, found its unerring way to his desk. Whether in his view it was important or trivial made no difference to the way in which he dealt with it – to the best of his very considerable ability.

Progressing as he did from office boy to clerk, from personal assistant and secretary to Mr William, to office manager, company secretary and director of the public company, Charles carried with him the aura of one who was single-minded in pursuit of diligence and excellence at every step. What also marked him out as an exceptional man was his charm and kindness. He not only participated fully in the life of the family he served throughout his business career, but also devoted himself wholeheartedly to his domestic responsibilities as a family man. Happily he is still with us, and continues to take an interest in the firm's progress.

Lest the reader should feel that this short account of the contributions of the non-family directors – and those of George Filby described later on – is over-full of superlatives, it should be stressed that a wrong impression would result were it otherwise. The family directors all feel that if they have any reason to congratulate themselves it is upon their choice of the men who have managed the company. In times of prosperity and of hardship these men have given of their best. Who could ask for more?

By 1962 David had also been made one of the joint managing directors, and Jeremy and Bruce were directors, and they, too, were drawn into the deliberations as to which direction the firm should take. As the directors saw it they had three choices: stay in shipping only and take the rough with the smooth; diversify, with the risks that entailed; or liquidate. Faced with these choices some would have understandably clung to what they knew, while others might have thought it better to get out while the going was good. Instead, the board chose unanimously to diversify. One area was insurance; the other was into Airtech's type of business.

Diversification as a matter of board policy was first mentioned in the firm's 1961 annual report, but it was not until August 1963 that the first acquisition was made by the public company when a 65 per cent interest was bought in an old-established firm of Lloyds insurance brokers owned by E. R. (Ronny) Wood, who was a friend of George Talbot Willcox. As soon as the purchase was completed E. R. Wood took Henry Head's place as Ropners' insurance brokers at Lloyds, just as in 1956 Eggar, Forrester had taken over the sale and purchase of Ropner ships from Thomas Pinkney.

Amongst the activities of one of the small northern insurance companies that had been bought up to form Ropner Insurance Brokers in 1960 was a hire-purchase business, and in 1963 this was incorporated as Greylands Finance Ltd, a hire-purchase company specializing in financing those who wanted to buy cars on hire purchase. Although a few fingers were burned – cars are not as good a risk as they should be – this venture went reasonably well for a number of years and at one time had several hundred clients. Eventually, it arrived at a point where the decision had to be made either to expand it into a nationwide hire-purchase company, with all the investment that would entail, or to stay small and go into another part of the financing market. The latter decision was arrived at and Greylands Finance Ltd started to lend on second mortgages. This proved much more successful as the security was better and the operation could be kept small and local. Later on, however, while working with a company building housing estates in the Northeast, the investment required again looked as if it would exceed what the directors thought reasonable. At one time upwards of £½ million was on loan against the security of various housing estates.

At the present Greylands Finance Ltd is not active, but at the time it did show the directors that investing in property could be relatively safe and profitable, and this had a bearing on their thinking when further diversification was planned. Before it ceased to trade Leonard's son, John, who had joined the firm in 1958 before working for five years with accountants Peat, Marwick, took over responsibility for it and ran it very successfully during the latter half of the 1960s. Through contacts in Malta he established Greylands Finance (Malta) Ltd, which financed the construction of several blocks of flats on the island. These proved very successful and all were sold. In October 1968 Ropner (Australia) Pty Ltd was incorporated in Perth, Western Australia, to fund a similar venture, which was completed in 1975. Again, all the apartments and houses built were sold successfully, but apart from these, and a joint venture converting an apartment block in Houston, Texas, entered into in 1979, Ropners has always invested in property in Britain.

After the purchase of E. R. Wood the next major acquisition occurred when Sir Eric Ohlsen approached the Ropner board on behalf of the remaining Airtech shareholders about the possibility of Ropners buying them out. It was decided that the fairest method of dealing with the situation was for the other shareholders to find the highest bidder for all Airtech's shares. If Ropners decided to equal, but not exceed, this bid then the other shareholders would agree to sell their shares to Ropners. If Ropners decided not to equal the bid the directors undertook to sell all Ropners' Airtech shares along with the others. A bidder was found, Ropners decided to equal it and 94 per cent of Airtech was acquired by August 1964, the balance being bought up soon afterwards.

Although Airtech's profits, along with those of Airvert and Hozelock, were still modest at that time, the purchase of the shares in these three companies was still a substantial investment for Ropners and the decision to buy them was certainly the biggest single one the board had ever had to make outside its shipping interests.

In June 1964 Guy retired as a full-time director, though he continued to work at the office in the mornings, and William Wiley and Charles Ringwood were elected to the main board. The same year Leonard gave up his seat in Parliament – serving in the Artillery through two world wars had badly affected his hearing – and so was able to devote more of his time to the firm, and he became the firm's new chairman. David, however, felt that with Leonard moving back to Darlington, and with a continuing programme of diversification taking place away from the Northeast, Ropners needed stronger representation in London. Like his father, he was interested in the work of the Chamber of Shipping and Lloyds' Register of Shipping, and with Ropners now having financial control of E. R. Wood and Eggar, Forrester, and the London shipbroking office expanding to include the broking agency of overseas companies like the Thyssen-owned Halcyon Lijn and Vulcaan, the presence of one of the family was needed in the City. So in 1965 he moved to London, but continued to visit Darlington on a regular basis.

By this time other members of the fourth generation had also found their niches in the firm. Jeremy, after working for a while with Eggar, Forrester, followed in his father's footsteps by concentrating on Ropners' shipping interests. Bruce, although he had started on the shipping side and felt very committed to it, became attracted to the engineering side, represented at that time by

Airtech, Airvert and Hozelock. In the fullness of time he too stepped into his father's shoes and became the chairman of Airtech Investments, the holding company for the Haddenham-based firms. John's interests lay first in Greylands Finance Ltd and Elton Stores and later in property, which is now such an important part of Ropners. However, all three worked in the same room, as their fathers had done before them, so there was, as there is today, close consultation between them on all aspects of the business.

Throughout the early 1960s the BOECC/Eggar, Forrester group continued to expand and by 1966 it needed more capital than the existing shareholders were prepared to sanction. As a result Peter Talbot Willcox bought the shipbroking subsidiary, Eggar, Forrester and Verner Ltd and Ropners ceased to have an interest in this part of the group – though Eggar, Forrester still handles the sale and purchase of some Ropner ships. The rest of the group was now renamed BOECC (Holdings) Ltd. Most of the Ropner (London) shares were bought by Ropner Holdings, which now had a 38 per cent shareholding in the new company. However, it was decided in the long term not to remain in BOECC and by 1971, when it changed its name to London American Finance Corporation, Ropners' percentage had dropped to under 3 per cent. However, Jock remained on the board until the last shares were sold in 1977.

With Hozelock doing particularly well in a larger factory and with an increasing range of garden products, it was felt that an expansion into other garden equipment should be made, so in 1968 Mills Tools, a Sheffield garden-tool manufacturing company with two factories, was acquired. It was hoped that its products would tie in with those of Hozelock's and that this would make it profitable. It was run until 1973, but proved unprofitable and was then sold to Stanley Tools at a price which recouped the original cost. Another unsatisfactory investment was the acquisition in 1967 of 51 per cent of a group of small companies supplying plastics and building materials. Euromarket Ltd traded for not much more than a year before it was decided to liquidate it, with the resultant loss to the firm of £450,000. Hard lessons were learned from both these ventures and for some years the directors concentrated their efforts in this field on expanding the basically profitable companies based at Haddenham, and in this they had considerable success.

In 1968 the remaining 35 per cent of E. R. Wood was bought, and the following year 100 per cent of another Lloyds broking firm, Bleichroeder, Bing & Co. Ltd was acquired. It had an office in Leeds which was combined with Ropner Insurance Brokers, and its life and pensions department was later enlarged to become Ropner Life and Pensions Ltd. The rest of the newly acquired company was merged with E. R. Wood. In 1970 Pool Insurance Holdings was created as the holding company for Ropners' insurance interests, and in January 1972 Ropner Insurance Services Ltd took over the combined Lloyds insurance broking business from E. R. Wood & Co. Ltd, and Bleichroeder, Bing & Co., and was housed in the latter's offices in Boundary House, Jewry Street.

The same year as Bleichroder, Bing was acquired it was decided by the board, after being advised by Rothschilds on the matter, that the time had come for the public company, Ropner Holdings, to absorb the private companies owned by the family directors as it was felt that family interests should not be involved with the public company.

'Again, it was a fairly major decision,' commented a director, 'as it meant that the holding company became masters of their own fate and it meant, too, that the family were employed by a public company not a private family one.'

This significant step was accomplished the following year, 1973, and was accompanied by some important changes amongst the directors. Leonard, William Wiley and Charles Ringwood retired from the board, and John, Bill Gidley, George Filby and John Baxter – a chartered accountant who had joined the firm in 1967 as Charles Ringwood's successor-elect as Financial Director – came onto it. The board elected a chairman, Robert, who unfortunately had to retire because of ill health in 1973. His place was taken by David, whose father, Guy, had died in 1971. Both Leonard and Robert died in 1977, and Jock retired in 1979. The only addition to the board since 1970 has been Max Gladwyn. He joined the firm in April 1981 from Hambro's Bank Ltd. He became a group director in 1982, a bridge between the fourth and fifth generation of Ropners, giving the firm the continuity of experience that is needed.

The next step to have important consequences occurred the same year, 1970. Sydney Codling, always on the lookout for new products, especially as contracts with the RAF had been reduced because of defence cuts, met an electronics expert, Professor George Sinclair of Toronto University, and introduced him to the Ropner family. The professor ran a small business, Sinclair Radio Laboratories Ltd, in Toronto and he suggested Ropners might be interested in investing in the company which was in the process of manufacturing advanced aerials, called multicouplers, for warships. This equipment, which enabled up to twelve channels of communication to be fed through two antennae stacked on top of one another, was allied to the kind of work with which Airtech had been traditionally involved. So a licence was obtained from Sinclair Radio Laboratories to manufacture multicouplers at Airtech's factory and sell them on a royalty basis, and in January 1974 a 25 per cent holding in the Canadian firm was acquired by Airtech. This was later increased to 33.3 per cent after Ropner Investments (Canada) Ltd had been formed as the holding company for the shares which were acquired from Airtech in December 1980.

During the 1970s Airtech proceeded to adapt the multicoupler to the rigorous requirements of the Royal Navy, and to the even more rigorous ones of some of the NATO navies. This they did very successfully, supplying the Dutch Navy with such an advanced design that, when the 1979 Fastnet yacht disaster occurred, only a Dutch warship, *Overijssel*, the guardship during the race, had a sufficiently sophisticated multicoupler to deal with the huge amount of communications traffic created by coordinating the search and rescue operation which involved yachts, ships, helicopters, aircraft, lifeboats and the coastguard. 'I would say that since 1975 the multicoupler is the single most successful product Airtech has had,' said a director; at the time of writing another large order for it has just been received.

In addition to the multicoupler, which Airtech is now developing for civilian as well as military use, a subcontract was signed in the early 1980s which uses Airtech's expertise in the field of systems engineering to put together a mobile communications system called Ptarmigan for the Army. The main contractor, Plessey, assembles the parts, which are then sent to Airtech for installation in one of several air transportable or vehicle transportable containers manufactured by Airtech.

According to Sydney Codling,

Airtech now consists of the communications container side which does projects like Ptarmigan and direct work with the Army and the RAF. That is about half the business. The other half is manufacturing electronics equipment in various forms. More and more of this we are making to our own design but quite a lot of it is still built to government specifications. We're looking all the time for new products to develop. In 1982 Airtech made a profit of about £3 million on a turnover of £11 million. Hozelock and Airvert were originally started to take away Airtech's dependence on government contracts, but they are now set up as independent entities so that Airtech is back where it was and I am concerned about its dependence on government work. Ptarmigan represents about 30–40 per cent of our workload over the next four or five years, but we still have to fill the remaining capacity to make Airtech profitable. We represent half the turnover of the group and about 80 per cent of the profits. I would like to see Airtech get into the commercial electronics field where it wasn't so dependent on government contracts. It's easy to say, it's not so easy to achieve.

Success brings its own problems, but the upsurge in Airtech and its subsidiaries during the 1970s is one of the most remarkable aspects of the Ropner story. Both Hozelock and Airvert now export to over sixty countries, and this accounts for between 30 and 40 per cent of their sales.

In 1968 a decision was taken to enter the property market in Britain, and as a first step John arranged for Greylands Finance Ltd to take a shareholding in a property company already established involving a firm of chartered surveyors, Lane Fox and Partners, and the Sheffield family (members of whom are directors of Portal Holdings). The property company was renamed Greytown Properties Ltd. However, Ropner liked what they saw of property developing activities and wished to expand their interest in this field. Consequently in 1970 a new company, Second Greytown Properties Ltd, a subsidiary of Ropner Holdings, was formed with the continuing participation of the Sheffield family and Martin Lane Fox, and Ropner agreed to provide substantial additional finance to support increased activities.

Martin Lane Fox's experience was, and is, in selecting the right opportunities and putting together complicated development deals to form key sites to build on, let, and then sell as going concerns.

The association between him and Ropners worked extremely well and continues to do so.

Meanwhile Portal Holdings had continued to operate separately, in conjunction with Martin Lane Fox, a property development company called the Laverstoke Property Company Ltd, but in 1973, as they had decided to withdraw from the property market, they sold their majority interest in Laverstoke to Ropners, who changed its name to Third Greytown Properties Ltd. Simultaneously, the Sheffield family relinquished its interest in the first two property companies.

The group continued to expand, and it was decided to establish a property investment company in addition to the three property dealing companies already operating. Greytown Investments was formed in 1973 for this purpose and, in order to establish a cohesive group, Greytown Property Holdings was also formed in 1973 to hold the shares in all four companies, which became subsidiaries of it.

To provide for further expansion, beyond the means of Ropner alone to finance, an arrangement was made with a Jessel subsidiary, London Indemnity and General Insurance Co. Ltd, to provide up to £10 million of additional finance in return for interest on the loan and a 20 per cent shareholding in Greytown Property Holdings Ltd. Under this arrangement Ropner and Martin Lane Fox each held 40 per cent of the holding company's shares.

About half of the agreed loan of £10 million had been obtained and invested in new property construction when the property crash of 1974 prevented London Indemnity from fulfilling its contractual agreement by lending the balance. However, the official receiver was persuaded to release sufficient funds for the completion of a number of half-built properties, but for a couple of years it was, as George Filby put it, rather a strain. But the crisis was weathered and, with confidence restored, a new company, Greytown Estates Ltd, financed solely by Ropners to build and sell commercial properties in the south of England, was formed in partnership with Lane Fox in 1976.

A family director commented:

The survival of that crisis and the subsequent development of the Property Development Division owes much to George Filby's skilled attentions, as does the success of the Insurance Broking Division which has operated for many years in the fast-changing environment of that industry, and which has continually needed adjustments and improvements to its structure.

George Filby joined Mainsforth Terrace as the new office boy in 1932. As with Charles Ringwood before him (though there must have been several office boys between them) it was improbable that anyone suspected the impact he would make in future years. It was a time of hardship and under-employment in West Hartlepool and George had been pleased to get the job. At the time this book is being written he is still working for the company; the fiftieth anniversary of his joining Ropners was celebrated with a large dinnerparty at Sir John's house, Thorp Perrow, in February 1982. It is only marginally true that George has taken life a little easier since then, but the time he has spent with the company (interrupted as it was by war service in the Army) has been crammed with more work and activity than most men see in a full lifetime.

The fact that George is still active in business, apart from making this vignette more difficult to write, also ensures that it is incomplete. It has seemed that there is nothing that George has ever been unwilling, still less incompetent, to take on. At the outset of the diversification programme, which was destined to relieve the group's dependence upon purely shipping activities, George was manager of the insurance and claims department which he had taken over at the time of Percy Dyer's death in 1955, but during the 1960s his adaptability, breadth of vision and willingness to undertake anything required of him were to ensure that he would play a prominent role in the future expansion of the company's business.

Greylands Finance Company was the first diversified operation to benefit from George's attention and it was from that foundation that the Property Development Division ultimately grew and prospered – although not without some hard-pressed times along the route. In parallel with these demanding activities, and with his involvement in the Insurance Broking Division, George continued to play a crucial role in the shipping side of the company. As is related elsewhere in these pages, the chartering emphasis swung from predominantly short-term operations to charters of considerable length. As the transition progressed, his expert knowledge of shipping practice and documentation was to prove invaluable during the lengthy and detailed negotiations which became a regular feature of the business.

George was elected to the board of the public company in 1970; the areas of its business which have not benefited from his boundless energy and knowledge of commercial procedure are few indeed and the full value of his contribution impossible to calculate.

During the latter half of the 1970s Greytown Holdings sold off all the properties it was involved in, and it has now been liquidated. In the meantime a new property dealing company called Greytown Estates Ltd had been formed in 1976 and had commenced trading. In 1982 a property investment company, Greytown Investments Ltd, was then formed to own Bunnian Place, Basingstoke, a large office development to be completed in 1985 and which is to be held as an investment. It is now the holding company for three other recently formed companies, Greytown Properties Ltd, Second Greytown Properties Ltd and Rotunda Properties Ltd, which are 60 per cent owned by Ropners and 40 per cent by Lane Fox. Properties under construction at the time of writing, or recently completed, include factories at Thurcroft, offices at Aylesbury, Hove, Oxford, Brighton and Bromley, and warehouses at Newbury and Southampton. In the financial year ending March 1982 the trading profit on the sale of development properties was £530,000, and in his statement to shareholders David remarked that first-class shop, office and industrial properties were continuing to be developed in the south of England and that Ropners' 'level of involvement in this market remains very active'.

From modest beginnings and with some minor reverses behind it the Property Division is playing an increasing part in the firm's prosperity.

During the latter part of the 1970s further expansion in the Engineering and Insurance Divisions took place. In November 1978 the whole equity of Frederick Greenwood and Sons (Holdings) Ltd, a Rochdale engineering group, was acquired. This had three separate companies which owned factories manufacturing different products and which were independent companies under the holding company.

Meltog Ltd, which has its factory at Driglington, near Bradford, produces can-making machinery suitable for export to Third World countries, while the Phoenix Ironworks, situated just outside Rochdale, manufactures heavy rollers for the paper-making industry. Frederick Greenwood itself originally manufactured parts for carpet looms, but with local carpet manufacturing badly hit by the current recession it diversified into making night storage heaters called Storad which are sold to the various electricity boards and to house builders such as Barratt Homes. The storage heaters now account for about half its turnover. Fifteen per cent of sales still comes from manufacturing parts for the carpet-making industry (it used to be 80 per cent) and the balance is made up from subcontract work, mostly making electrical light fittings. Initially a very profitable organization, it survived the recent recession and is now even stronger than before.

The Engineering Division's largest and most important acquisition since its inception came in 1983 with the purchase of Associated Sprayers Ltd, a major British company manufacturing garden equipment. Its acquisition was prompted by the fact that, although Hozelock had diversified during the 1970s into such products as small pumps for fountains and low-voltage floodlighting for garden pools and small gardens, it was still at the mercy of the weather. 'For about eight months of the year,' said a director, 'the managing director, David Codling, does all he can to manage the factory economically and efficiently, but for the other four months the man in charge is God. He decides if we're going to make a profit, not David Codling!'

By acquiring Associated Sprayers Ltd Hozelock's base was widened – they are now run as one company with a common administration, marketing and sales force. 'We've eyed Associated Sprayers for fifteen years,' said a director, 'and twice we've been very close to buying them. In September 1982 we failed again, but then, after watching them almost daily, we decided in December 1982 we must try very hard indeed to buy them, and we eventually did for just over £3 million. It's an excellent company, the leading garden sprayer firm in Britain, but it also manufactures other products like wheelbarrows and stepladders, and I feel it holds out great prospects.'

On the insurance side Ropners backed the formation of Henschien Insurance Services in Bergen, Norway, in 1974 and retains a sizeable interest in them. Two years later another life and pensions company, Estridge and Ropner Ltd, was started in Manchester and became an 80 per cent subsidiary of Ropner Holdings. In 1980 the two life and pensions companies were merged and renamed

Estridge and Ropner Life and Pensions Services Ltd, which is a subsidiary of Ropner Insurance Holdings Ltd.

Another profitable area of insurance was covered in 1977 with the formation, in partnership with Andrew Hall, of Hall, Ropner Ltd, a company specializing in bloodstock insurance in which Ropners hold 51 per cent. Andrew Hall is the son of Robin Hall, one of E. R. Wood's directors at the time it was bought by Ropners and subsequently its managing director.

In 1978 another small insurance broking firm, John Tyrie & Co., was acquired. It continued to trade separately for a number of years but is now being wound up, The same year, 1978, Morton Lindley, the managing director of Ropner Insurance Services, retired because of ill health and his place was taken by John Bennett and Garry Ropner, Bruce's younger brother, who had started his career in Henry Head before moving to E. R. Wood. The marine side of the business continued to do well, but the non-marine and motor side needed strengthening. So in 1981 a new joint company, Ropner and Ireland Ltd, was formed with another firm of Lloyds brokers, T. L. Ireland, and Tim Ireland now runs the UK non-marine business with Ropner taking a share in the brokerage. Also in 1981 Michael Tucker and some colleagues from his previous firm joined Ropner to form a specialist reinsurance broking company.

The recent changes and acquisitions on the insurance side have now created a dynamic division of growing importance.

Despite such an active and successful programme of diversification in Great Britain some of the directors have always been keen to invest in the United States of America.

Through Bruce's brother, Garry Ropner, such an opportunity arose. A joint venture with Robert J. Arnold, an old friend of Garry's, has been formed in the reinsurance field. The company named Ropner and Arnold was incorporated in New York towards the end of 1985 and specialises in reinsurance operations from a New York based office.

This new company is seen as a fine complement to the existing insurance broking network which now embraces companies in London and Darlington in the UK as well as Norway, Holland and New York.

13
Shipowners Still

No mention was made in the last chapter of the progress of the shipping division during the 1960s and 1970s, though it is very much part of the modern conglomerate – indeed, in some ways its backbone. It has been left to last because not only does it seem appropriate to finish the Ropner story with what for more than a century was the firm's *raison d'être* but because shipping is still in some intangible way the bedrock on which Ropners continues to stand. Shipping may not make the profits it has in the past – though in the future it may do again – but tradition dies hard in the Northeast and affection for the industry which brought Ropners into existence is undiminished within the firm. Perhaps loyalty plays a part in sticking with it, but so does the hard fact that so far as capital employed is concerned the industry is still the firm's mainstream business.

The last survivor of the prewar fleet, *Wearpool*, was sold to the Rex Shipping Company of Stockholm in 1954. Thirteen of the fifteen war-built ships acquired after the cessation of hostilities were also sold during that decade. The first four new building contracts placed by the company after the war were for the liners *Daleby*, *Deerpool*, *Somersby* and *Swiftpool* previously mentioned.

On completion of the liner programme the two tankers and three vessels intended for the tramp business were ordered. These last were *Troutpool* (1956), of similar size to the war-built tonnage, and, in 1957, *Romanby* and *Rushpool* were delivered by Sir James Laing of Sunderland. *Troutpool* was to have a relatively short life of seven years with the company but *Romanby* and *Rushpool*, each of 14,480 t.d.w., were very successful ships, having been built to an advanced design with bridge amidships and engine aft, hitherto a feature applied mainly to tankers. *Romanby* was time-chartered for a period of five years following delivery to Vulcaan of Rotterdam, old friends of the company, and in view of the slump which soon followed she proved to be a most valuable profit-earner during that time.

Following the closure of the Gulf Line, *Somersby* earned her keep on the tramp market for a short period but was sold in 1958 when the Admiralty identified her as a potential fleet auxiliary and offered a generous price. The directors decided that a replacement should be found and advantage was taken of an offer from the Finnboda Shipyard of Stockholm. *Willowpool*, 12,950 t.d.w., the last ship with machinery amidships to be ordered by the company, was launched the following year.

The occasion was attended by unusual circumstances in that when the launch party were ready to leave their hotel the shipyard manager arrived in the foyer where they were assembled and announced, 'The ship is launched.' On the not unreasonable assumption that the gentleman's command of the English language was less than perfect, Jock, whose wife was to name the ship, smiled politely and affirmed that the party was ready to go. It transpired, however, that the ship really was launched, having descended the slipway without benefit of formal sanction. Fortunately, there had been no injury or damage and the naming ceremony took place alongside the fitting-out berth.

In the meantime there had been a further and most significant addition to the fleet. This was *Wandby*, a 17,170 t.d.w. bulk carrier with both engines and bridge aft. Larger still than the two Laing ships and of single-deck construction, she was to prove an easily tradable and most successful ship. But, despite the acquisitions mentioned above, the fleet had grown smaller in terms of number of units and in the decade of the 1960s it was to diminish further still.

The market slump of the early 1960s was the deepest and most prolonged of any since the war. The directors decided to dispose of the oldest, least economical ships remaining in the fleet, believing, as it proved correctly, that their profitable trading days were over. Accordingly the last two remaining war-built ships, *Levenpool* and

Swainby (Ropner's last steamers – the end of a long line) were sold in 1962; the original liner-types *Daleby* and *Deerpool* had been sold a year earlier. These sales were followed by those of *Troutpool* in 1963 and *Swiftpool* in 1964.

Nevertheless the directors pursued the policy of their forebears and ordered new ships when it seemed that prices could sink no lower. In 1962 they took delivery of *Bridgepool*, a sister vessel to the successful *Wandby*, and *Barlby*, a bulk carrier of 24,870 t.d.w. After a short pause for breath they went on to order *Stonepool*. She was delivered in 1966 and was, at 45,027 t.d.w., by far the largest ship in the fleet – in fact, one of very few of her size afloat at that time. She was unique to Ropners in that she had twin funnels sited side by side aft. But, despite these investments, some far-reaching changes in the company's shipping philosophy were imminent.

In 1966, having effectively carried responsibility for the company's shipping operations since the outbreak of war in 1939, Jock decided that the time was right to relinquish day-by-day control to the younger generation. David had responsibility for the direction of the London end of the business and so Jeremy and Bruce were given charge of the ships. In the event it was soon found that Bruce was most useful in the fast expanding engineering enterprise, although his time with the ships gave him experience which was later to be valuable at board level.

Following the sale that year of the tanker *Thornaby*, the fleet in 1966 consisted of *Romanby*, *Rushpool*, the tanker *Thirlby* (on long-term charter to Shell) *Wandby*, *Willowpool*, *Bridgepool*, *Barlby* and *Stonepool* – eight units, of which seven (the dry-cargo ships) were employed upon short-term charters.

Jeremy was instructed by the board not to place too much reliance on opportunism in the spot market and to adopt a somewhat defensive stance. For some considerable time past Jock had noted the advantage conferred by a timely fixture of one or more years in the period market and this prudent policy was now continued and intensified whenever the market seemed propitious. Some useful contacts were made in the Far East at this time. However, *Willowpool* proved to be a difficult ship to trade and she was sold in 1967. *Barlby* had been mainly employed in the US Gulf-Europe grain trade but was less successful in the time charter market. The board decided that she should be sold and she left the fleet in 1968, followed by *Romanby* and *Rushpool* in 1969 and 1970 respectively. In view of the subsequent rise in the market, these sales proved to have been prematurely timed. However, the company was now considering the longer term market and it was not feasible for suitable charters to be found for these ships.

In 1966 Jeremy was introduced by Peter Talbot Willcox to the Skaugen Shipping family of Oslo who, together with the Ruud-Pedersen, Morland and Tonnevold companies, were members of the Norwegian Bulk Carriers Consortium. The Consortium was a highly successful enterprise specializing in the contracting of iron ore and other bulk cargoes principally for European steel producers. It was assembled and subsequently managed by Mr Jan Poulsen, an experienced and successful Oslo broker, with the help and support of the owners concerned. This contact was to have far-reaching consequences. Soon afterwards negotiations began for the construction and chartering out to N.B.C. of two 106,490 t.d.w. bulk carriers. These charters were signed after long, intricate negotiations had taken place and included a profit-sharing element to Ropner based upon the results of the voyages undertaken on behalf of N.B.C. Both ships were built by Harland and Wolff of Belfast in 1971 and marked the beginning of a mutually profitable ongoing association with N.B.C.

Following the sale of the fleet's last between-decker, *Rushpool*, in 1970, its strength pending delivery of the two Harland and Wolff new buildings was reduced to an all-time low of four ships. *Thirlby* continued to serve her charter with Shell, the sister ships *Wandby* and *Bridgepool* traded profitably, as did *Stonepool*, despite earlier misgivings about her size (soon proved unfounded). The board, however, did not trust the strength of the market and *Wandby* was sold in 1972.

Boom conditions, into which the promising prospects of the late-1960s had subsequently blossomed, brought in their train a spate of orders from overconfident speculators as well as from the more conservative owners, including the N.B.C. members who ordered a total of five new ships: two 129,000 t.d.w. ore/oil carriers from the Kawasaki Shipyard in Japan and three bulkers of 117,000 t.d.w. from Harland and Wolff. One of these, a Harland and Wolff ship, was to be owned by Ropner and entered in (as opposed to chartered to) the Consortium.

The market remained buoyant until 1974 and then, reflecting the decline in world trade brought about by the oil crisis of 1973, fell like a stone. Worldwide shipping profits, save for vessels chartered out before the crisis, dwindled to vanishing point and the flood of ships released onto a bare market could find little to do; many were immediately laid up. Ropners, however, were relatively securely placed. Three of the five-ship fleet had been chartered out before the cataclysm. But the board considered that stern measures were called for, and *Bridgepool*, which had been a most successful ship, was promptly sold. Her original price had been so low that the company was still able to realize a book profit from her disposal.

The 117,000 t.d.w. bulk carrier which had originally been ordered for entry in the N.B.C. Consortium and launched in 1977 as *Otterpool* was instead chartered to the British Steel Corporation for fifteen years and renamed *Lackenby*, an old Ropner name but also the name of a major B.S.C. installation on the River Tees. A second similar ship was purchased whilst under construction at Harland and Wolff for a Norwegian company; she was named *Appleby* and chartered to B.S.C. on terms similar to those of *Lackenby* in 1978.

Besides its mainstream activities, the company maintained its shipbroking business in London and its ship management business on behalf of other owners. For the Western Canada Shipping Co. Ropners managed *Mossel Bay* from 1950 to 1954, *Walvis Bay* from 1950 to 1957, *Lake Kootenay* from 1954 to 1957, *Lake Atlin* from 1956 to 1965 and *Lake Burnaby* from 1957 to 1958. In 1960 and 1961 respectively two small refrigerated ships, *Golden Comet* and *Silver Comet*, were placed under Ropner management by Mr Antonio Bonny, a Canary Island tomato grower of Spanish ancestry and Swiss nationality whom Jeremy had first met in Stockholm. The ships were built in Holland and registered in Guernsey. Such is the cosmopolitan nature of the shipping business!

In 1961 *Lady Esme*, a 90-foot ferry boat, was constructed by Phillip & Sons Ltd of Dartmouth for use in the Seychelles Islands as part of a development deal arranged by Leonard. Five years later the Seychelles Government purchased the boat which (in 1985) is still in service.

The London broking office lost its broking agency for the Halcyon Lijn and Vulcaan at the time of the reorganization of the

Thyssen empire, but established an active and remunerative relationship with the short-sea owners Comben Longstaff, a subsidiary of Consolidated Goldfields. With encouragement from Ropner London these owners later decided to enter the deep-sea trade and ordered two 30,000 t.d.w. bulk carriers. This association prospered for some years, during which Mr Chris Jackson of the London office took care of the broking needs of both companies, Ropner and Comben Longstaff, but came to an end when Consolidated Goldfields decided to withdraw from shipowning altogether in 1981.

Another company for which Ropner London provided broking services was Stag Line of North Shields. Ropners had enjoyed a cordial relationship with this very old-established company, which was managed by the Robinson family, for many years and had purchased a modest shareholding in it in 1972. By 1974 this holding had been increased to a little less than 30 per cent of the company and Jeremy was invited to join the Stag Line board. The relationship expanded to encompass a combined approach to crewing and other administrative matters along with the broking arrangement. In 1979 Bruce was asked to join the board too, and Ropners were considering making an outright bid for the capital of the company when, in 1981, a third company with strong northeastern associations, Huntings, made an offer for the shares which Ropners were not willing to match. Huntings' bid was therefore accepted and a substantial profit was realized on the deal.

Throughout the period covered in this chapter the company maintained – and continues to do so in the 1980s – a very strong technical department headed successively by Mr R. J. Gates, Mr J. E. Church and Mr E. Cherry. The greatest importance was attached to ship design and supervision of the shipyards during construction. In addition to being amongst the leaders in terms of the increased size of ships built, the company were also amongst the innovators in relation to economy of operation, engine-room auxiliaries and machinery layout. Special attention was given to ensuring that officers and crew accommodation was comfortable and convenient and that there were comprehensive navigational aids and labour-saving equipment on deck. The directors consider that this policy has ensured a minimum of time (and therefore hire) loss for the ships and a maximum of operational efficiency.

Ropners have had the fortune to be well served by their shore staff, and their seagoing staff have been no less efficient and conscientious. It would be invidious to list names because too many would have to be left out to make the list readable, but nevertheless no history of the company could disregard mention of Captain J. Kenny and Captain C. H. Churchill who each commanded the company's first new ships since the war, the purpose-built liners *Daleby* and *Deerpool*, and who each, along with many others, gave the company year after year of loyal and skilled service.

In 1980 and 1981 the shipping market enjoyed a short-lived period of relative prosperity. *Rudby*'s charter with N.B.C. had given the charterers the option of selling the vessel after five years – with a subsequent division of any proceeds in excess of book value – and in 1980 they very sensibly availed themselves of the opportunity afforded by the strength of the market and realized a handsome profit.

After twenty-three years of unbroken service to Shell the gallant *Thirlby* finally outlived her usefulness to them and was released from her charter. No opportunity could be found for her elsewhere and consequently she was sold. She had been a steady if unspectacular source of revenue and seafarers' employment throughout her term and was sadly missed when she went in 1981. *Stonepool*, another ship which had given long and distinguished service, was sold in 1982; she was replaced by a similar-sized vessel which had originally been contracted at the Eleusis Shipyard in Greece by a Greek owner. Work on the berth had ceased pending an improvement in demand for such ships but the shipyard recommenced construction when the company bought the contract at a reduced price. She was delivered in 1982 and named *Salmonpool*. In the same year Ropners purchased two 27,000 t.d.w. bulk carriers which had been delivered by the Hakodate Dock Co. to Rethymnis and Kulukundis in 1974 and chartered to B.H.P. of Australia for fifteen years. These were *Iron Kestrel* and *Iron Kerry* (renamed *Iron Kirby*). Each had more than half of her charter left to run and it was considered that they would make a valuable contribution to the profitability of the fleet.

The company's management business was under some pressure at this time since no less than three of the company's ships were based in Australia and had to be manned in that country. This was to an extent mitigated when Ropner Management Ltd was given the management of *Ravenscraig*, a sister ship to *Lackenby* and *Appleby*, and another slightly larger vessel, *Farland*, was entrusted to them by Skaarup Shipping Corporation of Greenwich, USA, on behalf of Swedish owners. The revenue which accrued from this extra work enabled the company to maintain a fully efficient shipping staff in Darlington at a time when the Ropner fleet by itself would not have been economically able to support one.

Appendix I The Ropner Fleet

ACQUIRED	NAME	DWT
1874	Amy	800
	Shotton	1,100
	Seaton	1,350
	Magdeburg	1,450
	Wave	1,450
	Lufra	1,950
	Renpor	1,925
1876	Hesleden	2,300
1877	Horden	2,350
	Helmstedt	2,350
1878	Crimdon	2,500
	Elpis	2,950
1879	Harsley	2,500
	Eden	2,050
1880	Parklands	2,500
	Blackhalls	1,600
	Lufra (2)	2,500
	Hardwick	1,600
1882	Preston	3,750
	Wellfield	2,800
	Watlington	2,700
	Hartburn	2,810

ACQUIRED	NAME	DWT
1883	Renpor (2)	2,810
	Gledholt	2,450
1885	Greystoke	3,100
	Preston (2)	3,100
1887	Wave (2)	3,600
	Alicia	2,100
	Romanby	2,500
	Sowerby	1,800
	Picton	3,600
1888	Elton	3,900
	Crathorne	4,350
	Hurworth	3,600
	Swainby	4,100
	Tarpeia	2,600
1889	Leven	3,600
	Maltby	4,350
	Thornaby	2,600
	Aislaby	4,350
	Raisby	3,300
1890	Ormesby	4,350
	Newby	3,300
1891	Kirkby	4,550
1892	Slingsby	4,500
	Haxby	5,000
	Skidby	5,500
1893	Roxby	4,700
1894	Busby	4,800
	Lackenby	3,155
1895	Carperby	3,155
	Hawnby	3,200
	Selby	3,200

ACQUIRED	NAME	DWT
1895	Granby	2,900
	Barlby	3,680
1896	Ashby	2,950
	Moorby	3,900
	Trunkby	4,000
	Yearby	4,000
1897	Oakby	3,000
1898	Tenby	6,700
	Bellerby	4,735
	Thirlby	3,050
	Mountby	4,750
1899	Wandby	6,700
	Gadsby	4,400
1900	Glenby	3,075
	Daleby	6,175
	Dromonby	6,175
	Wragby	6,000
1901	Westonby	6,100
	Tolesby	6,250
1903	Heronspool	5,700
	Therese Heymann	3,650
	Troutpool	5,210
1904	Hartlepool	7,480
	Swainby (2)	6,600
1905	Burnby	6,600
	Brookby	6,600
	Stagpool	7,480
	Teespool	7,480
1906	Rollesby	6,700
	Maltby (2)	6,700
	Millpool	6,940

ACQUIRED	NAME	DWT
1907	Clearpool	6,940
	Ingleby	6,110
	Coleby	6,700
1908	Romanby (2)	6,750
	Teesdale	3,680
1909	Pikepool	6,260
	Martin	2,900
	Holtby	6,260
1910	Spilsby	6,260
1911	Levenpool	8,750
	Scawby	6,580
1912	Rockpool	8,080
	Fishpool	8,083
	Willerby	6,580
1913	Salmonpool	8,660
	Somersby	6,580
	Wearpool	8,675
	Baldersby	6,580
	Seapool	8,080
1914	Saxilby	6,580
1917	Swainby (3)	8,825
1918	Sedgepool	9,400
1923	Roxby (2)	7,680
1924	Salmonpool (2)	8,570
	Bridgepool	8,570
	Reedpool	8,600
	Rudby	8,670
	Drakepool	8,600
1925	Willowpool	8,600
	Ainderby	8,670

ACQUIRED	NAME	DWT
1926	Firby	8,670
	Otterpool	8,670
1927	Warlaby	8,670
	Troutpool (2)	8,695
	Romanby (2)	8,670
	Rockpool (2)	8,650
	Ullapool	8,650
	Ashby (2)	8,660
1928	Mansepool	8,650
	Thirlby (2)	8,650
	Gullpool	8,660
	Hindpool	8,650
	Carperby (2)	8,650
	Kirkpool	8,730
	Lackenby	9,030
	Stonepool	8,670
	Cragpool	9,100
	Rushpool	9,030
	Boulderpool	8,670
1929	Heronspool (2)	9,150
	Haxby (2)	9,150
	Swiftpool	9,110
	Yearby (2)	10,100
1930	Deerpool	9,130
	Somersby (2)	9,130
1931	Canby	7,930
	Coalby	7,883
1932	Domby	9,060
1934	Daleby (2)	8,935
1935	Stagpool (2)	7,370
	Clearpool (2)	9,370
1936	Moorby (2)	9,160

ACQUIRED	NAME	DWT
1936	Hawnby (2)	9,300
	Wearpool (2)	9,160
	Alderpool	8,275
1937	Eastpool	6,330
	Danby	7,600
1940	Seapool (2)	9,283
	Fishpool (2)	9,568
	Wandby (2)	9,560
1945	Clearpool (3)	9,744
	Levenpool (2)	10,521
	Swainby (4)	9,751
	Thirlby (3)	9,570
1946	Bellerby (2)	10,150
	Cedarpool	10,456
	Preston (3)	5,219
1947	Firby (2)	10,490
	Ingleby	10,490
	Oakby (2)	10,490
	Pikepool (2)	10,490
	Teespool (2)	10,490
	Hurworth (2)	10,666
	Rudby (2)	10,859
	Sedgepool (2)	10,531
1949	Heronspool (3)	10,490
1950	Daleby (3)	7,846
	Deerpool (2)	7,846
1954	Somersby (3)	9,290
	Swiftpool (2)	9,870
1955	Thornaby (2)	18,270
1956	Troutpool (3)	10,212
1957	Romanby (4)	14,480
	Rushpool (2)	14,480

ACQUIRED	NAME	DWT
1958	Thirlby (4)	20,996
1959	Wandby (3)	17,170
1960	Willowpool (2)	12,950
1961	Lady Esmé	Ferry
1962	Barlby (2)	24,870
	Bridgepool (2)	17,312
1966	Stonepool (2)	45,027
1971	Rudby (3)	106,490
	Iron Somersby	106,490
1977	Lackenby	117,366
1978	Appleby	117,613
1982	Iron Kilby	26,868
	Iron Kestrel	26,419
	Salmonpool (2)	43,108

Appendix II The Ropner Family Tree

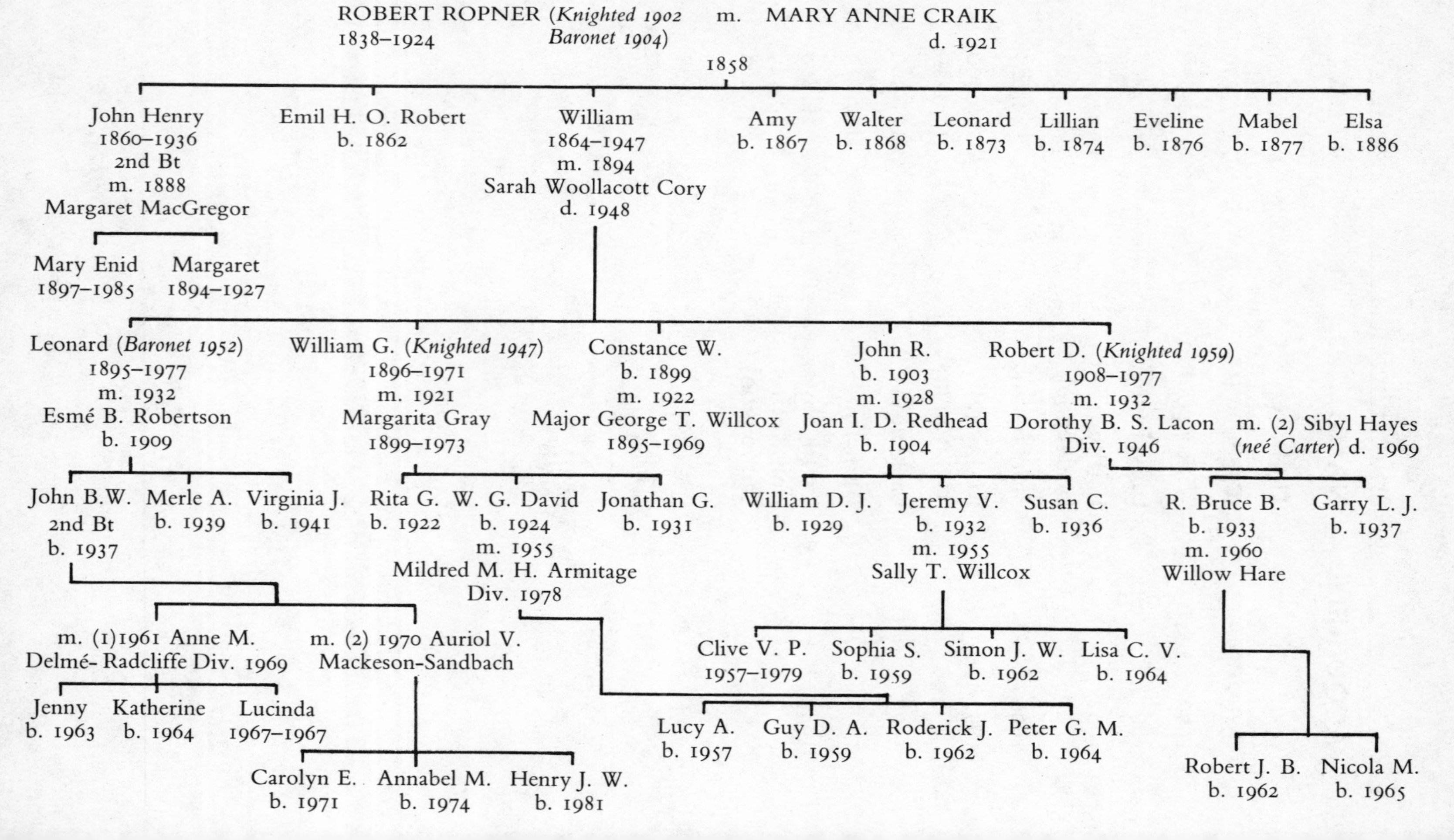

Appendix III Companies and Directors of the Ropner Group

Robert Ropner & Co (formed 1875)

	Joined	Appointed	
Robert Ropner (*founder*)			
J. H. Ropner		1886	
Wm Ropner		1891	
(*a partnership*)			

Sir R. Ropner & Co Ltd (formed 1915)

	Joined	Appointed	
Robert Ropner	1875	1915	
J. H. Ropner	1886	1915	
Wm Ropner	1891	1915	
Wm C. White	1892	1915	Died 1921
Thos Barker	1894	1915	Died 1938
Leonard Ropner	1919	1922	Retired 1975
William Guy Ropner	1919	1922	Died 1971
John Raymond Ropner	1925	1928	Retired 1976
Robert Desmond Ropner	1930	1935	Retired 1975
Percy Whitfield Dyer	1906	1951	Died 1955
William Guy David Ropner	1947	1953	
William Wiley Jnr	1915	1954	Retired 1965
Charles Ringwood	1916	1954	Retired 1976
Jeremy Vyvyan Ropner	1952	1958	
Robert Bruce Beecroft Ropner	1958	1960	
John Ropner	1958	1964	

	Joined	Appointed	
William George Gidley	1930	1965	Retired 1976
William George Filby	1932	1965	Retired 1985

Ropner plc (incorporated 1948)

Col Sir Leonard Ropner Bt	1919	1948	Resigned 1970
John Raymond Ropner	1925	1948	Resigned 1979
Sir Robert Ropner	1930	1948	Resigned 1975
Sir William Ropner	1919	1948	Resigned 1964
William Guy David Ropner	1947	1953	
Jeremy Vyvyan Ropner	1952	1958	
Robert Bruce Beecroft Ropner	1954	1960	
William Wiley Jnr	1915	1964	Resigned 1970
Charles Ringwood	1916	1964	Resigned 1970
Sir John Ropner Bt	1958	1970	
William George Gidley	1930	1970	Resigned 1976
William George Filby	1932	1970	
J. C. Baxter	1967	1970	
M. J. Gladwyn	1981	1983	

Index

Adelaide, 66
Adele Traber, 99
Admiral Hipper, 88
Admiralty, 38, 39, 40, 82, 83, 136
Africa, 92
Ainderby, 61, 63, 66, 67–73, 91
'Aircon' containers, 117
Airtech Ltd, 114–17, 118–19, 120, 123, 125, 126, 128–9
Airtech Investments, 126
Airvert Ltd, 118, 125, 126, 129, 133
Aislaby, 25
Alderpool, 89–90
Alexandria, 11, 95
Alicia, 19–20
Allen, J. Sandeman, 41–2
Alvis, 116
Amy, 5–6, 16, 18, 24
Antonia, 68
Appam, 39
Appleby, 139, 142
Appleby, Ropner & Co., 5–7, 9–11
Appleby, Thomas, 3–5, 7, 9–11, 54
Archangel, 96
Arnold, Robert J., 134
Arras, 56
Arundel, Captain, 85
Ascania, 67
Ashby, 39, 93
Ashby (2), 61
Associated Sprayers Ltd, 133
Atkinson, Captain, 86–7, 99
Atlantic Ocean, 39, 66–73, 77–81, 86, 88, 89, 91, 93–5
Austin, Captain, 46
Austin, Miss, 57
Australia, 16, 31, 59, 60, 100, 105, 124, 141
Austria, 40
Aviation Traders, 115
Avonmouth, 19, 44
Aylesbury, 132
Azores, 88

Bahr, Behrend, 104
Baldersby, 50–1
Baldoyo Bank, 65
Baltic Exchange, 21, 121–2
Baltic Sea, 3, 12, 42
Barker, T., 52, 53, 57, 74
Barkston Ash, 74
Barlby, 137–8
Barratt Homes, 133
Barrow-in-Furness, 96
Barry Roads, 81
Bartlett, Captain F. J., 37
Basingstoke, 132
Batonne, 40
Batson, Captain, 77–8
Battersby, W. F., 52, 57
Baty, Captain, 95
Baxter, John, 127

Beaven, W. W. J., 41
Bedale Hunt, 15
Beddington, Isaac, 12
Bedlington, 23
Belfast, 138
Belfast Lough, 86
Belgian Relief Committee, 38
Bell Rock, 85
Belle Isle wireless station, 66
Bellerby, 98
Benghazi, 96
Bennett, John, 134
Berengaria, 66
Bergen, 133
Berlin, 50
Berlin Airlift, 114, 115
Berner, Captain F. C., 66
Bessel, Emilie, 1–2
Bestell, Captain E., 67–73
B.H.P., 141
Bilbao, 41
Birch, Captain, 89–91
Birchleaf, 49
Biscay, Bay of, 11, 40, 41, 66
Black Sea, 31
Blackhalls, 13
Blairangus, 86
Bleichroder, Bing & Co. Ltd, 127
Blogg, George Henry, 41
Blücher, 35
Board of Transport Control, 100–1
BOECC (Holdings) Ltd, 126
Boer War, 28
Bombay, 42
Bona, 84, 85
Bonny, Antonio, 139
Bordeaux, 85
Boulderpool, 89
Boyd Weir and Sewell, 104
BP, 111
Brackenbury, Captain, 10
Brandenburg, 49
Brand's Patent Pulverised Fuel Company, 62
Brazil, 91
Breeze, 7
Bremen, 104
Bremerhaven, 87
Bricquette Island, 55
Bridgepool, 61, 89, 96, 98
Bridgepool (2), 137, 138, 139
Brighton, 132
Brigitte, 99
Bristol Channel, 38, 40, 48, 80, 86
British-American Air Services, 115
British Army, 100, 101, 102, 117, 128–9, 131
British Columbia, 88
British Overseas Engineering Credit Company (BOECC), 119, 126
British Red Cross Sailors Society, 50
British Shipping (Assistance) Act (1935), 75
British South American Airlines Corporation, 115–16
British Steel Corporation, 140
Brittany, 102
Brockett, Captain J., 39
Bromley, 132
Brookby, 45
Brooklands, 56
Brown Jenkinson, 104
Buenos Aires, 93
Bunnian Place, Basingstoke, 132
Burnaby, 40

California, 15, 134–5
Cambridge University, 56, 64
Canada, 63–4 92, 98, 101, 128
Canby, 64
Cape Verde Islands, 35, 79, 89
Cape Wrath, 99
Cardiff, 13, 17, 21–3, 25, 26, 38, 40, 54, 100, 102
Carperby, 93
Castle Eden, 4, 8

Castle Eden Volunteers, 12
Cedarpool, 98
Chamber of Shipping, 27–8, 30, 74, 97, 101–2, 103, 106–7, 120, 125
Chard, Captain J. N., 46
Chartair Ltd, 113–15, 118
Cherry, E., 141
Chobham, 117
Church, J. E., 141
Churchill, Captain C. H., 89, 95, 96–7, 142
Clare College, Cambridge, 56
Clearpool, 63, 77, 91–2, 98
Clematis, 23
Cleveland, 28
Clouston, Mr, 102
Clyde, Firth of, 88, 91, 96
Coalby, 63–4
Codling, David, 133
Codling, Sydney, 114–18, 127–9
Cole, Captain, 96
Coleby, 36–7
Comben Longstaff, 140
Common Brothers, 112
Conservative Party, 28, 56
Consolidated Goldfields, 140
Convoy Division, 101
Copping, Captain, 92
Corpus Christi, 85
Corunna, 65
Coverdale and Sons, 23
Cragpool, 98
Cranfield Aeronautical College, 116
Crathorne, 24
Crighton, Captain William, 36
Crimdon, 13
Crippled Children's League, 33, 108
Criton, 92
Cronstadt, 7, 42
Croydon, 114
Cunard, 67, 68, 103
Dalbek, 99
Dale, 47
Daleby, 44
Daleby (2), 89, 95
Daleby (3), 104–5, 135, 137, 141
Danby, 98
Danube, River, 31
Danzig, 66
Darlington, 1, 102, 125, 134, 142
Dartmouth, 46, 139
Davies, Fireman, 44
Davison, A., 47
Deane, Harry, 56
Deep Sea Tramp Negotiating Committee, 101
Deerpool, 66, 84
Deerpool (2), 104–5, 135, 137, 141
Denton, Gray & Co., 5–6
Depression, 54–64, 74–5
Devonport, 45
Dogger Bank, Battle of the, 35
Domby, 64, 98
Dominion Coal Company, 63–4
Dover Castle, 56
Dow, Mr, 102
Downs, 39
Downs, Captain, 95
Drakepool, 61, 98
Driglington, 132
Dromonby, 39
Dublin, 47, 103
Dunkirk, 42
Durham, 26, 27, 32–3
Durham School, 22
Durham Volunteer Regiment, 12, 33
Dutch Navy, 128
Dyer, Percy, 52, 56, 74, 112, 121, 131

Eagle Aviation, 115
Eden, 13
Edward, Prince of Wales, 109
Eggar, Norman, 119
Eggar, Forrester, 123–4, 125, 126

Eggar, Forrester and Verner Ltd, 103, 104, 119, 126
Elcomb, F. W., 21, 25
Eleusis Shipyard, 141
Elmbank, 86, 87
Elpis, 13
Elton, 24
Elton Stores, 111–12, 126
Elwick, 108
Empire Arnold, 95 102
Empire Bison, 88
Empire Cabot, 98
Empire Clarion, 98
Empire Dryden, 93
Empire Grange, 97
Empire Irving, 98
Empire Lionel, 98
Empire Merlin, 88
Empire Mombasa, 99
Empire Moonrise, 93
Empire Mouflon, 98
Empire Rainbow, 95
Empire Salmonpool, 87–8
Empire Starlight, 93–4
Empire Sunbeam, 98
Empire Tide, 98
Empire Trent, 88
Essex Yeomanry Field Regiment, 101
Estridge and Ropner Ltd, 133–4
Estridge and Ropner Life and Pension Services Ltd, 134
Euromarket Ltd, 126
Evans, Captain D., 39
Eves, Captain, 50–1
Ewe, Loch, 91

Fair Isles, 47
Falmouth, 45
Far East, 31, 137
Farland, 143
Fastnet, 45, 67, 72, 128
Fearless, 77
Filby, George, 102, 112, 113, 123, 127, 130–2
Filey, 35
Finnboda Shipyard, 136
Firby, 61, 77, 80, 99
First World War, 34–8, 39–51, 54–5, 56
Fishpool, 95–6
Fisker, Captain M. A., 38
Flannel Islands, 47
Flores, Isle of, 93
Folkestone, 37
Forestry Commission, 100
Forges et Chantier, 98
Forrester, Vassall, 103, 119
Fort Gauges, 50
Fort George, 95
Fort Pelly, 95
Fort Zorndorf, 50
France, 56, 66, 92, 102
Frank, Captain, 93
Freemasons, 8
Frost, Captain J. T., 38
Furness, Withy, 54

Gadsby, 38
Gardiner, Captain, 93
Garston, 44
Gates, R. J., 140
Geipels, 3
General Council of British Shipping, 101
General Strike (1926), 59, 60
Genoa, 58
George Pyman, 5
German High Seas Fleet, 35
Germanicus, 55
Germany, 1–3, 22, 53, 55, 100; First World War, 35–8, 39–51; Second World War, 73, 75–83, 84–97
Gibraltar, 40, 45, 46, 47, 58, 85
Gichner Mobile System, 117
Gidley, Bill, 102, 103, 121–2, 127
Girdwood, Mr, 37
Gironde, 98
Gitania, 1, 2

Gladwyn, Max, 127
Glasgow, 85
Gledholt, 19
Glenby, 38
Golden Comet, 139
Gothenburg, 1
Grace, Charles, 11
Granger, Captain Ben, 10, 12
Gray, William, 6
Gray, William & Co., 7, 19, 21, 22, 23–4, 61, 62, 77
Greece, 6, 142
Green, Captain J. W., 45
Green, Milton, 118
Green, Pete, 118
Green, Captain Samuel, 39
Greenland, 92
Greenwood, Frederick and Sons (Holdings) Ltd, 132–3
Greylands, 102
Greylands Finance Ltd, 124, 126, 129, 131
Greylands Finance (Malta) Ltd, 124
Greystoke, 16, 19
Greytown Estates Ltd, 130, 132
Greytown Investments Ltd, 130, 132
Greytown Properties Ltd, 129, 132
Greytown Property Holdings, 130, 132
Guernsey, 140
Gulf Line (Ropner Line), 103–5, 106, 110, 119, 122, 136
Gulf of Mexico/Continent Conference, 104
Gulf of Mexico/UK Conference, 104
Gullpool, 92, 98, 106

Haddenham, 114, 118, 126
Hain, 68
Haisboro' Buoy, 89
Hakodate Dock Co., 141
Halcyon Lijn, 102, 125, 139–40
Halifax, 88, 89
Hall, Andrew, 134
Hall, Robin, 134
Hall, Ropner Ltd, 134
Hambro's Bank Ltd, 119, 127
Hamburg, 1, 2
Hamburg Line, 85
Handley, Mr, 102
Hansard, 28
Hanwell, 114
Hardwick, 7, 8
Hardwick (2), 13
Hardwick Hall, Castle Eden, 8
Harland, Captain, 81–2, 86, 88
Harland and Wolff, 138, 139
Harsley, 13
Harrow School, 56
Hartburn, 19
Hartlepool, 1, 2–8, 13, 35
Hartlepool, 55
Hartlepool Port and Harbour Commission, 27, 33, 109
Hartlepools Shipowners' Society, 27
Hartlepools Shipping Federation, 27
Haswell, Shotton and Easington Coal Company, 12, 14
Hawnby, 34
Hawnby (2), 63, 86, 88
Haxby, 85
Hayster, Able Seaman Frederick, 81
Head, Henry Ltd, 112, 123, 134
Helmstedt, 2
Helmstedt, 13
Henry, Mr, 87
Henschien Insurance Services, 133
Heronspool, 34
Heronspool (2), 62, 77–8, 80
Heronspool (3), 99
Hesleden, 13
Hewison, Captain, 96
Hewison, Captain W., 38
Hill, Captain, 96

Hill, Captain T. M., 42–4
Hindpool, 89
Hitler, Adolf, 97
Hoffman, J., 13–14, 21
Holland, 49, 102, 128, 139
Holtby, 63
Home Guard, 101
Hord, Captain Charles, 44
Horden, 13
Hornfels, 55
Hospitals of London Combined Appeal, 109
House of Commons, 4, 28, 56–7, 72, 74–5, 82, 110
Houston, Texas, 104, 124
Hove, 132
Hozelock Ltd, 117–18, 125, 126, 129, 133
Hudson Bay, 77
Huelva, 44
Hull, 84, 104
Humber, River, 84, 92
Hunting Percival, 116
Huntings, 141
Hurworth, 24, 99
Hutton Rudby, 28

Indian Ocean, 66
Ingleby, 99
Ireland, 43, 44, 47, 66
Ireland, T. L. Ltd, 134
Ireland, Tim, 134
Iron Kerry, 141
Iron Kestrel, 141
Iron Kirby, 141
Irvine's Shipbuilding and Dry Docks Co., 61
Israel, 115
Istanbul, 58

Jackson, Chris, 76–7, 102, 140
Jackson, E. W., 43
Japan, 94, 138
Jessel, 130
Jones, D. M., 22
Jones, Captain J. E., 40

Kamouraska, 63–4
Karlsruhe, 50
Kattegat, 47–8
Kawasaki Shipyard, 138
Kennebunk, Maine, 65
Kennington, Captain, 94
Kenny, Captain J., 141
Kentish Knock, 38
Kerston Miles, 99
Kiel, 48
Kiel Canal, 48
Kimmins, Simon, 119
Kingsland, S. F., 45
Kirby, W., 52, 74
Kirkby, 38
Kirkpool, 94
Korean War, 99
Kronprinz Wilhelm, 36–7

Labour Party, 56
Lackenby, 95
Lackenby (2), 139, 142
Lady Esme, 139
Laing, Sir James and Sons, 104, 135
Lake Atlin, 139
Lake Burnaby, 139
Lake Kootenay, 139
Laker, Sir Freddie, 115
Lambert Brothers Ltd, 113, 116, 118
Lancashire, 7, 100
Lancaster, W., 13, 52, 57
Land Tenure Act, 28
Lane Fox, Martin, 129–30
Lane Fox and Partners, 129, 132
Laverstoke Property Company Ltd, 130
Leask, Clark & Co., 34
Leeds, 113, 127
Lerwick, 45, 46

Levenpool, 31, 38
Levenpool (2), 98, 136–7
Lights Advisory Committee, 29
Lindley, Morton, 134
Little Cumbrae Island, 88
Liverpool, 103
Liverpool Underwriters' Association, 41–2
Lloyds, 11, 20, 41, 84, 94, 112, 113, 123, 127, 134
Lloyds' Register of Shipping, 27, 31, 103, 125
London, 13, 17, 21, 25, 26, 76, 102, 103, 104, 107, 109, 125, 134, 139–40
London American Finance Corporation, 126
London Indemnity and General Insurance Co. Ltd, 130
Londonderry, Lord, 28
Loos, 56
Luckhurst, Mr, 2
Lufra, 7, 9, 11, 23
Lufra (2), 13
Luftwaffe, 89
Lundy Island, 82

McKenzie, Captain Donald, 45–6
Magdala, 6, 7, 9–10
Magdeburg, 12
Magdeburg, 6, 9, 10, 11
Mainsforth Investments Ltd, 112
Malta, 50, 124
Maltby, 25, 47
Manchester, 88, 103, 133–4
Mansepool, 88
Marbella, 39
Marryat, Frederick, 2
Marseilles, 35
Marshall Aid, 104
Martin, 34, 40
Matthews, Jack, 116
Maughan, Captain B., 45
May, 6
Mayo, Bob, 116
Mediterranean, 38, 40, 46, 47
Meltog Ltd, 132
Merchant Shipping Acts, 7, 29, 34
Merchant Ships Awards Committee, 44, 46
Merseyside, 89, 100, 104
Mexico, Gulf of, 103
Miami, 104
Middle East, 95
Middlesbrough, 84
Middleton, Robert Morton Jr, 19–20
Milford Haven, 46, 48
Millpool, 66–7, 68, 69
Mills Tools, 126
Ministry of Defence, 116–17
Ministry of Shipping, 77, 82, 88, 89, 93, 101
Ministry of Supply, 100
Ministry of War Transport, 84, 88, 98–9, 101–2
Moewe, 39
Moltke, 35
Montgomery, Field Marshal Viscount, 97
Montreal, 58, 60, 66, 67, 88, 103
Moorby, 63, 98, 104
Morgan, Chief Engineer B., 94
Morgan, Mr, 102
Morland Co., 138
Mossel Basy, 140
Mountby, 46–7, 50
Mumbles, 72
Murmansk, 93

Narvik, 87
NATO, 128
Nazis, 73, 77, 84
New Elton Stores, 112
New Orleans, 47, 104
New York, 19, 38, 78, 103, 104, 134
Newbury, 132
Newcastle, 8, 14, 112

Newcastle Journal, 75
Newfoundland, 65, 81, 86
Newport, 22, 41
Newton, Captain, 66–7
Niarchos, Stavros, 120
Nicholson, Captain, 87
Nicholson, J., 52
Normandy landings, 101
North Atlantic Liner Conference, 104
North of England Indemnity Association, 11
North of England P. & I. (Protection and Indemnity) Association, 11, 120
North of England Protecting Club, 11
North of England Steamship Insurance Association, 11
North Sea, 47
North Shields, 141
Northeast Railway Company, 56
Norway, 53, 58, 85, 87, 133, 134, 138, 139
Norwegian Bulk Carriers Consortium (N.B.C.), 138, 139, 141

Oakby, 37, 99
Ocean Fame, 99
Ocean Pilgrim, 99
Ocean Pride, 99
Ocean Valour, 99
Ocean Vanity, 99
Ocean Vengeance, 99
O'Dair, Mr, 111
Ohlsen, Sir Eric, 118, 119, 124–5
Ohlsen Steamship Company, 118
Olive, Captain John, 47
Onaway, 61
Orion, 85
Orkney, 47
Ormesby, 42
Oslo, 139
Otterpool, 61, 66, 85
Otterpool (2), 139
Overijssel, 128
Owens, Captain William, 39
Oxford, 132

Paola, 23
Parklands, 13
Pearse, Matthew & Co., 19, 24
Pearson, Able Seaman George, 78
Peat, Marwick, 124
Pepel, 89
Perth, Australia, 124
Pescoe camp, 50
Phillip & Sons Ltd, 139
Phoenix Ironworks, 132–3
Picton, 21
Pikepool, 43–4, 86–7
Pikepool (2), 99
Pile, Spence & Co., 1, 5
Pinkney, Thomas, 123–4
Plate, River, 31, 35, 105
Plessey, 128
Plumbium Manufacturing Corporation, 118
Pool Insurance Holdings, 127
Pool Shipping Company, 33–4, 38, 53, 54, 58–60, 65, 75, 98, 109, 113–14
Port Augusta, 95
Port Talbot, 66
Portal Holdings, 129, 130
Portland, 44
Poulsen, Jan, 138
Prawle Point, 45
President Harding, 78
Preston, 19, 21
Preston (2), 19, 24
Preston (3), 98
Preston Hall, 14–15
Preston Shipping Company, 98
Prince, Captain, 77, 85
Prinz Eitel Friedrich, 35–6
Prussian, 48
Ptarmigan communications system, 128–9

Putsig, 87
Pyman, George, 54

Queenstown, 72

Raisby, 25
Ravenscraig, 142
Read, James, 7
Reardon Smith, William and Sons Ltd, 25
Redcar, 43
Reedpool, 61, 95
Reliance, 89
Renpor, 9, 11, 14
Renpor (2), 19
Rethymnis and Kulukundis, 141
Rex Shipping Company, 135
Riddy, Mr, 102
Ringwood, Charles, 12, 57–8, 74, 121, 122–3, 125, 127, 131
Roberts, Captain, 49–50
Robinson, Captain, 95
Robinson, Stanley, 37
Robinson family, 140
Rochdale, 132
Rockpool, 47
Rockpool (2), 61, 63, 81–2, 86, 88
Rollesby, 45–6
Romanby, 19–20, 46
Romanby (3), 61, 87
Romanby (4), 20, 135–6, 137–8
Rooke, Captain, 10
Ropner, Amy, 4, 5
Ropner, Bruce, 64, 118–19, 123, 125–6, 133–4, 137, 140
Ropner, Constance Winsome, 32, 113
Ropner, David, *see* Ropner, William Guy David
Ropner, Elsa, 12
Ropner, Emil Hugo Oscar Robert (Robert Jr), 4, 24, 30, 32, 64
Ropner, Eveline, 12
Ropner, Garry, 64, 134
Ropner, Guy, *see* Ropner, Sir William Guy
Ropner, Jeremy, 64, 101, 123, 125, 137–8, 139, 140
Ropner, Jock, *see* Ropner, John Raymond
Ropner, Sir John (son of Leonard), 15, 64, 124, 126, 127, 129, 131
Ropner, John Henry (Robert's father), 1–2, 12
Ropner, Sir John Henry (Robert's son), 57, 108; childhood, 4; shipping business, 22, 30, 32, 34, 52, 55; partnership, 26; marriage, 32; in public life, 32–3; in the Depression, 60–1; modernization programme, 62–3
Ropner, John Raymond (Jock), 32, 112, 119, 121, 126, 136; joins Ropners, 64; marriage, 64; in the Depression, 74, 75; in the Second World War, 77, 101–2; after the war, 103, 105; postwar problems, 107–8; closes Gulf Line, 110; retirement, 127, 137
Ropner, Leonard (son of Sir Robert), 8, 24, 74
Ropner, Sir Leonard (son of William), 32, 140; First World War, 35, 56; marriage, 64; political career, 56–7, 74–5, 103, 110, 125; in the Second World War, 82–3, 100; air transport, 113; retirement, 127; death, 127
Ropner, Lilian, 8
Ropner, Mabel, 12
Ropner, Margaret MacGregor, 32
Ropner, Margarita Gray, 6, 64
Ropner, Lady Mary, 3, 52
Ropner, Sir Robert, 1, 57, 60; early life, 1–4; first ships, 5–8,

Ropner, Sir Robert – *contd.* 17; sets up own business, 9–15, 16–18; expands business, 19–24; buys shipyard, 24–5; hands over to his sons, 26; in public life, 26–9; and the Chamber of Shipping, 27–8; Pool Shipping Company, 33; First World War, 37–8; last years, 52–3
Ropner, Sir Robert (son of Robert Jr), 32
Ropner, Sir Robert Desmond, 32, 74, 119–20; joins Ropners, 64; in the Second World War, 101–2; postwar problems, 99, 106–7; and the Ropner Line, 103; aviation interests, 113, 118; retirement, 127; death, 127
Ropner, Sarah Wollacott Cory, 32
Ropner, Walter, 8, 24
Ropner, William (son of Jock), 64
Ropner, William (son of Robert), 21–2, 24, 25, 57–8, 64, 74; childhood, 4; partnership, 26; shipping business, 30, 32, 34, 52, 55; marriage, 32; in public life, 33, 108–9; First World War, 35, 44; in the Depression, 60–1, 65, 75; modernization programme, 62–3; death, 108, 109
Ropner, Sir William Guy (Guy), 32, 97, 119; marriage, 6, 64; First World War, 35; joins Ropners, 56; in the Depression, 74, 75; in the Second World War, 89, 100–1; after the war, 103; postwar problems, 107; retirement, 125; death, 127
Ropner, William Guy David (David), 27, 28–9; 125, 127, 138; birth, 64; in the Second World War, 101; diversification, 123, 132, 134
Ropners: established, 9–15, 16–18; expansion of, 19–24, 30; passed on to Robert's sons, 26; types of vessels, 30–2; forms Pool Shipping Company, 33–4; in First World War, 34–8, 39–51, 54–5; reorganization, 53; in the Depression, 54–64, 74–5; modernization programme, 60–3; in the Second World War, 73, 75–83, 84–97, 100–2; postwar problems, 99, 105–9, 110; Gulf Line, 103–5, 110; oil tankers, 110–11; Elton Stores, 111–12; aviation interests, 113–17, 118; diversification, 123–34; postwar shipping, 135–42
'Ropner's Navy', 40–2, 83, 84
Ropner, Sir R. & Co. Ltd, 53, 98, 109
Ropner, Sir R. & Co. (Management) Ltd, 109
Ropner and Arnold Ltd, 134
Ropner and Ireland Ltd, 134
Ropner (Australia) Pty Ltd, 124
Ropner Holdings Ltd, 109, 112, 119, 126, 127, 129, 133
Ropner Insurance Agency, 112–13
Ropner Insurance Brokers, 113, 124, 127, 131
Ropner Insurance Holdings Ltd, 134
Ropner Insurance Services Ltd, 64, 127, 134
Ropner Investments (Canada) Ltd, 128
Ropner Life and Pensions Ltd, 127
Ropner Line (Gulf Line), 103–5, 106, 110, 119, 122, 137
Ropner (London), 119, 126
Ropner Management Ltd, 142
Ropner Record, 105
Ropner Shipbuilding Company, 61

Ropner Shipping Company, 53, 59–60, 64, 65, 75, 98, 109, 113–14
Rosario, 36
Rothschilds, 119, 127
Rotterdam, 38, 136
Rotunda Properties Ltd, 132
Rouen, 43
Roxby (2), 61, 95
Royal Air Force (RAF), 102, 116–17, 128, 129
Royal Artillery, 101, 125
Royal Canadian Air Force, 116
Royal Navy, 83, 101, 102, 128
Rudby, 61
Rudby (2), 99, 106, 141
Rushpool, 88
Rushpool (2), 136–7, 137–8
Russia, 93–4
Ruud-Pedersen, 138

Sagunto, 45
St George's Channel, 38
St Helen's Lodge, 8
St Lawrence, Gulf of, 55, 77
St Petersburg, 1, 10
Salcombe, 45
Salisbury Green, D., 118
Salmonpool, 39–40, 61, 87–8
Salmonpool (2), 141
Sam Suva, 96–7
Sam Sylarna, 96
Sam Tay, 99
Samdart, 99
Samlistar, 99
Samuel, Captain B. J., 66
Sanderson, Mr, 23
Savona, 35
Saxilby, 34, 50, 63, 66
Scarborough, 35
Scawby, 38
Scilly Isles, 45, 85
Scotland, 38
Scott, Walter, 14
Seapool, 98
Seaton, 6, 9, 11, 12
Second Greytown Properties Ltd, 129, 132
Second World War, 73, 75–83, 84–97, 100–2
Sedgefield, 56, 74, 76, 102
Sedgepool, 55, 88
Sedgepool (2), 99
Seidlitz, 35
Seine, River, 111
Selby, 34
Seychelles Islands, 139
SHAEF, 102
Shaw Brothers, 104
Sheffield, 126
Sheffield family, 129, 130
Shell, 111, 137, 138, 141
Sheriff, W. S., 43
Shinwell, Emanuel, 82
Shipping Airlines Ltd, 113
Shipping Federation, 1, 43, 44, 102
The Shipping World, 30
Short Bros., 7–8
Shotton, 6, 9, 10, 11
Sicily, 95, 97
Silver Comet, 140
Simpson, Captain David, 41–2, 88
Sinclair, George, 128
Sinclair Radio Laboratories Ltd, 128
Skaarup Shipping Corporation, 142
Skaugen Shipping, 138
Skitter Sands, 91–2
Skutterskelfe, 28
Smith, Captain W., 25
Somersby, 65
Somersby (2), 91
Somersby (3), 106, 110, 135, 136
Soundcraft Magnetics Ltd, 118
South Africa, 59
South America, 16, 31, 95
South Durham, 8
Southampton, 112, 132

Sowerby, 19–20
Spouse, Captain, 91
Spurn Point, 84
Stag, Hugh, 41
Stag Line, 140
Stagpool, 98
Stanley, J. F. R., 45
Stanley Tools, 126
Stein, Captain, 94
Stockholm, 136, 139
Stockton, 1, 14, 19, 24–5, 26–7, 29, 30–2, 34, 61
Stockton Conservative Party, 28
Stonepool, 63, 77, 78–81, 92
Stonepool (2), 137, 138, 141
Storad, 133
Strachan Shipping Company, 104
Suez Canal, 31, 120
Suez crisis (1956), 100
Sunderland, 104, 135
Sutton, C. V., 52
Swainby, 24
Swainby (2), 34, 55, 62, 87
Swainby (3), 98, 137
Swansea, 67, 72, 77
Sweden, 87, 143
Swiftpool, 62, 92
Swiftpool (2), 106, 135, 137
Symes, Mr, 102
Syracuse, 95

Tate, Captain, 95
Taylor, Woodrow, 119
Tees, River, 43, 45, 91, 139
Tees Conservancy Commission, 27
Teesdale, 34, 43, 45
Teespool, 46
Teespool (2), 99, 104
Tees-side, 113
Tenby, 42
Therese Heymann, 33, 35
Third Greytown Properties Ltd, 130
Thirlby, 42–3, 89, 90–1, 93
Thirlby (2), 98
Thirlby (3), 111, 137, 138, 141
Thompson, Captain, 91
Thompson, Captain R. W., 102
Thomson, Captain, 76
Thorn, J., 52
Thornaby, 27
Thornaby, 25, 39
Thornaby (2), 111, 137
Thurcroft, 132
Thurso, 77
Thwaites, Captain, 89
Thwaites, John C., 12, 13, 53
Thyssen, 125, 140
The Times, 37–8, 74, 82–3, 105, 108–9, 120
Tinnock, Captain, 89
Tonnage Replacement Scheme, 98, 106
Tonnevold Co., 138
Toronto, 128
Le Trait, 111
Tramp-Shipping Administrative Committee, 75
Tramp Standing Committee, 102
Transport Ship Licensing Committee, 102
Trematon, 68
Troutpool, 34, 61, 65, 86
Troutpool (2), 135, 137
Trunkby, 30, 39
Tucker, Michael, 134
Tunis, 40
Tyne, River, 25, 35, 38, 45, 46, 54, 58, 77, 89, 93
Tyrie, John & Co., 134

U-boats, 39–51, 73, 77–82, 85, 86–8, 89–90, 95, 97
Ullapool, 61, 89
United States of America, 16, 36, 37, 39, 53, 58, 95, 98–9, 100, 104, 117, 134
US Army, 102
Ushant, 39

Valentia radio station, 66
Vulcaan, 125, 136, 139–40

Wabana, 66
Wabana, 63–4
Wake, E., 43
Wales, 13, 43
Wall Street crash (1929), 63
Walvis Bay, 139
Wandby, 41–2, 65, 88
Wandby (2), 88
Wandby (3), 136, 137, 138
War Deer, 50
War Hind, 50
Ward Jackson, Ralph, 1
Warlaby, 61, 88
Watkins, ex-Colour-Sergeant Thomas, 82
Watlington, 19
Wave, 6–7, 9, 10
Wave (2), 21
Wearpool, 63, 98, 135
Wedgwood, Captain, 35–6
Wellfield, 19, 20–1
Welsh Guards, 118
West Hartlepool, 1, 2–8, 13, 21, 22, 24, 26, 33, 52, 54, 57, 76, 102, 131
West Hartlepool Dock and Railway Company, 1
West Hartlepool Steam Navigation Company, 54
Western Canada Shipping Co., 139
Westonby, 45
The Whins, 76
Whitby, 35
White, Captain, 79–81
White, F., 52
White, Captain John, 40, 47–50, 51
White, W. C., 52, 53
White Sea, 45
Wiley, William, 56, 74, 121, 122, 125, 127
Wilhelmina, Queen of the Netherlands, 102
Wilhelmshaven, 48
Willcox, George Talbot, 113–14, 116, 119, 123
Willcox, Peter Talbot, 119, 126, 138
Willerby, 35–6
Willowpool, 61, 84–5
Willowpool (2), 136, 137
Wilson, Gunner, 44
Wilson, Captain J. C., 40
Winga, 6
Withy, Ernest, 19, 21
Wood, E. R., 123, 124, 125, 127, 134
Wood, J. A. & Co., 34
Workers Compensation Act, 28, 34
Wragby, 40

Yare, Captain, 87
Yearby, 92, 96, 98
Yorkshire, 7, 27, 28
Young, Captain, 9
Ypres, 56